JEANNE D'ARC'S GRAND STRATEGY

FRED HAMBURG

ISBN 9789493056459 (paperback)

ISBN 9789493056466 (ebook)

Copyright © Fred Hamburg, 2020

Publisher: Amsterdam Publishers

info@amsterdampublishers.com

Illustrations: Erik Hamburg

All Rights Reserved. No part of this publication may be reproduced or transmitted in any form or by any means, electronic or mechanical, including photocopy, recording or any other information storage and retrieval system, without prior permission in writing from the publisher.

CONTENTS

Foreword	v
1. Jeanne's Life	1
2. The Siege of Orléans	7
3. The Loire Offensive	16
4. The March on Reims	23
5. The Coronation	26
6. The Journey to Paris	31
7. Jeanne's Attributes	39
8. Jeanne's General Skills	52
9. Jeanne's Military Skills	57
10. The Followers of La Pucelle	60
11. War in the Middle Ages	67
12. The French Army	75
13. Women in the Army	78
14. Jeanne d'Arc's Grand Strategy	84
15. Aspects of Jeanne's Tactics	106
16. Jeanne's Power	117
17. How did Jeanne obtain Power?	126
18. How did Jeanne lose Power?	131
19. Jeanne as a Leader	137
20. Jeanne as a Charismatic Commander	148
21. The Significance of Personality in War and Politics	155
Epilogue	158
Appendix I	163
Appendix II	167
Principal Characters	171
Bibliography	175

FOREWORD

In this book I comment on Jeanne d'Arc's leadership and strategy. Ideally, my analysis would be based on objective facts, but unfortunately not all events in Jeanne's life are well documented. Historians also interpret her life in different lights. For instance, Catholic scholars consider her to be one of the greatest saints in history, carrying out the will of God. [Or as some call her: a saint in which the actions of God became visible.[1]] More feminist authors, on the other hand, see Jeanne d'Arc as a confident girl who used a religious vocabulary to accomplish her own plans. Others believe they can diagnose the French heroine with various illnesses, like anorexia. Because I want to focus on Jeanne's leadership and strategic reasoning, it is not necessary to go over some of the disputed historical facts for the umpteenth time.

Not much is said in the testimonies of her contemporaries about Jeanne's strategic thinking or her charismatic leadership. With my book, I want to provoke some thought and discussion in this area. My book can therefore be considered a substantiated *interpolation* of available data.

Of course, I must and will examine the abilities of the great saint, especially where these are linked to her leadership. I will do this with the intention of finally highlighting the astonishing fact that Jeanne's followers, including the high-ranking officers of the Dauphin's army, passionately shared the beliefs of the Maid and were willing to fight themselves to death.

Leiden, 2020

---

1. Virion (1972), p.20.

'War allows, even demands, the most complete use of all man's faculties, physical as well as emotional and intellectual. (...) it enables those faculties to be employed against the most dangerous opponent: namely, another man who is as strong, and as intelligent, as oneself.' - Martin van Creveld

'Leadership (...) is the thing that wins battles. I have it – but I'll be damned if I can define it.' - General Patton

'The essence of ultimate decision remains impenetrable to the observer – often, indeed, to the decider himself.' - John F. Kennedy

1   JEANNE'S LIFE

'Joan: I heard voices telling me what to do.
They come from God.
Robert: They come from your imagination.
Joan: Of course.
That is how the messages of God come to us.'
- George Bernard Shaw's *Saint Joan*[1]

Jeanne d'Arc was born in 1412 in Domrémy (Lorraine) to less fortunate but not destitute Catholic peasants.[2] Jeanne was a simple girl, illiterate and remarkably pious. From her twelfth birthday she heard voices, in the first instance[3] only Archangel Michael, but later also Saint Catherine[4] and Saint Margaret.[5] These voices[6] taught her 'à se bien governer et frequenter l'église'.[7]

At one point[8] the archangel commanded the girl to bring Charles VII to the French throne. [Charles had been declared king but was not crowned and anointed for the English had conquered large parts of his country and had their own claim to the throne.] Jeanne's voices urged her to begin her mission by contacting Castellan Braudicourt of nearby Vaucouleurs, a nobleman who had remained faithful to the French king.

At this moment in time Charles VII had his seat in the Languedoc. It seemed impossible for the Dauphin to quickly reconquer the former centre of his kingdom.[9] *If the English were to conquer Orléans, they would control the Loire and directly threaten the Dauphin's headquarters in Chinon.*[10]

At the age of 16, the brave girl indeed goes to Vaucouleurs. She told everyone that she had to meet the Dauphin before Lent because she was bringing him help from heaven and that he did not have to seek it from others.[11] No wonder that everyone wanted to see this wondrous girl with her perplexing purpose.

After being rejected by Braudicourt twice, she finally leaves with his permission.[12] In a small company she travels – dressed in men's clothes – to the king.[13] After her arrival in Chinon, the suspicious Dauphin – through his helpers – asks Jeanne what brings her to him. The girl replies that she has come to lift the siege of Orléans and crown the king in Reims. The Dauphin decides to meet her (despite objections from his surroundings). He receives her in a large hall lit by fifty flaming torches alongside 300 knights.[14]

Not intimidated, Jeanne tells the king that she was sent by God to anoint and crown him as the true heir of le Saint Royaume.[15] Then she tells the king a secret that can only be known to him and God.[16] That revelation gave the Dauphin great confidence. It also tallied with the prophecy of Marie d'Avignon, who had predicted years before that there would come a virgin who would take up the sword to save France.[17] 'Jeanne La Pucelle,'[18] as our heroine from Domrémy now calls herself, is given shelter in one of the towers of the palace. Charles VII, who had initially taken her for 'une folle',[19] has the Maid examined by theologians and clerics to make sure that her intentions are pure.[20] She is investigated for weeks in Poitiers, where she is secretly observed by specially designated women. She passes all tests with flying colours.

Jeanne then enters the court circles. She gets from the king an outfit, horses and an entourage, that is to say: the company of her two brothers, an attendant, two pages and two couriers. The appointment of the latter alone refutes the assertion that the Maid was only a mascot as only high-ranking officers had a courier at this time. Her sword is found, following the instructions of the voices in her head, in the ground behind the altar of a church in Sainte-Catherine-de-Fierbois. It has, as predicted, five crosses on the scabbard. The girl from Domrémy is now officially co-commander of the army. Around this time, she dictates her *Lettre aux Anglais*.[21] It was her first order to the English to cease besieging Orléans, leave all occupied cities and return to England.

Meanwhile in Orléans, a rumour is going around that a young woman in men's clothing and a short hairstyle is on her way to the Dauphin to release the city with help from heaven. Within ten days of her arrival in Orléans, the impossible happens: the siege of Orléans is lifted. Capitalising on the momentum, the Maid then pleads for a coronation tour to Reims. This 'Loire offensive' gets off to a flying start and turns into a dazzling triumph. Charles VII can finally be crowned and anointed. Jeanne la Pucelle has now reached the zenith of her military career.

From this moment on, a coalition of schemers around the king push her out into the cold. She is, for example, kept unaware of a secret agreement between Charles VII and Philip of Burgundy[22], which causes the attack on Paris (which Jeanne favours) to be postponed.[23] The trip to the French capital is therefore long and winding and the attempt to take Paris fails. Charles withdraws to Gien and dissolves his army.

On her own initiative, Jeanne nevertheless undertakes an aid mission to royalist Compiègne. There she is captured by the Burgundians during a sortie and sold to the English. The English then organise a politically motivated show trial. Its purpose is to condemn La Pucelle to death as a heretic in order to undermine the conquests and pretensions of Charles VII. On 30 May 1431, she is burned at the stake.[24] In 1456 she is rehabilitated in the eyes of the Church and on 9 May, 1920 Jeanne d'Arc is canonised by Pope Benedict XV.

* * *

Q. How could it happen that an illiterate 17-year-old peasant girl becomes a commander of the king's army?

A. There was no rational, orthodox alternative anymore; everything had been tried and everything had failed. 'Only a regime that is desperate pays attention to an illiterate peasant daughter who claims to hear voices from God instructing her to take the lead of Charles VI's military machine and to carry it to victory.'[25] Or as Jean Barbin, a lawyer for the French Parliament, said: 'The King and the inhabitants who remained faithful to him were desperate at that time and did not know how to hope for help if it did not come from God.'[26]

1. Donald Spoto (2007) opens his *Joan: The Mysterious Life of the Heretic Who Became a Saint* with this citation.
2. Her parents enjoyed some regard in the local vicinity. Jeanne's father was a farmer and a labourer but also at some point – together with another inhabitant of Domrémy – a tenant of the 'castle' on the island near the town (which until two years before had been inhabited by Jean II of Bourlémont). Most researchers date Jeanne's birth to 1412. Heinz Thomas (2000) convincingly deems 1411 to be more probable.
3. Only during her trial would Jeanne declare that there was an Archangel Michael and later a Saint Catharine and a Saint Margaret; see the *Protocol of the interrogation* from 27 February 1431 (before that point in time she heard only 'voices').
4. Patron of the 'gottgefälliger Gelehrsamkeit' (Thomas, 2000), p.103.
5. Saint Margaret was rejected by her pagan father for her Catholic faith. She was put to death after refusing to marry the man her father had chosen for her.
6. Or were they visions? This debate started during her trial in Rouen. Her judges were less sympathetic to her visions than the people. Was this already a sign of disbelief? Or did this skepticism herald the advances of Protestantism?
7. 'To behave well and go to church often.'
8. This is the story Jeanne told in Rouen.
9. Thomas (2000)
10. DeVries (2011)
11. Pernoud & Clin (2011), p. 33. Loosely translated, Jeanne told Jean de Metz, one of her companions on her journey to the king, the following: 'There is indeed no one, no king, no duke, no daughter of the King of Scotland, nor anyone else, who may win back the kingdom of France; and there will also be no help unless from me. I would rather have stayed at home, spinning with my poor mother, because it is not in accordance with my state that I am going to do all this, but it is necessary that I go and do it, because my Lord wants me to do so.'
12. Braudicourt had given in to the support of the citizens of Vaucouleurs for Jeanne.
13. From Sainte-Catherine-de-Fierbois, on the final leg of her journey, Jeanne dictates a letter to the king.
14. There is also a theory according to which this meeting was preceded by a very informal one (with only a few advisers).
15. 'The Holy Kingdom.' One of Charles VII's problems was that he doubted his kingship since his mother, Isabella of Bavaria, had called him a bastard.
16. To date, no one knows exactly what was said. The promise of a sign before

the gates of Orléans? A revelation of the prayers of the king? Even during her trial, Jeanne was silent (or ambiguous) about this event.
17. See Pernoud & Clin (2011), p.40/41 and p.51.
18. 'Jeanne the Maid.'
19. Thomas (2000), p.107.
20. This is what some say, but others claim that Charles VII wanted to establish a reputation for purity in this manner, and for that reason decided to accompany her to Poitiers.
21. This letter was written on 22 March 1429 in Poitiers and sent from Blois between the 24 and 27 April.
22. Negotiations between the two had taken place since Orléans.
23. We now know that Charles VII was left hanging by Philip's peace proposals (as already Jeanne suspected). Only in 1435 did Philip make peace with Charles VII.
24. 'A premeditated judicial murder,' Fabre (1948, Dutch translation), p.305.
25. Richey (2000), p.20 of 32 of a downloaded file.
26. Cited in Pernoud & Clin (2011), p.51.

2 THE SIEGE OF ORLÉANS

'All men naturally shrink from pain and danger, and only incur their risk from some higher motive.'
- General Sherman

Friday, 29 April: Jeanne arrives from Blois with equipment and provisions. She had wanted to approach Orléans from the right bank, over La Beauce, but the commanders of the convoy[1] chose the other (Sologne) bank while pretending to agree with Jeanne's choice; at Chécy, Jeanne finds out that she has been deceived.[2]

Meanwhile, the French are faced with the problem of having to cross the river with their equipment while the wind and water levels are unfavourable. In the end, the transport succeeds only because suddenly – in line with Jeanne's prophecy – the wind turns so that the ships can collect and unload their cargo in time.[3]

La Pucelle, as Jeanne is now known everywhere, wanted – if possible - to attack the English immediately on arrival. But the Bastard of Orléans, in charge of the defence of the city, prefers a grand entry with Jeanne playing a key part. He thus goes against Jeanne's desire to stay - for the time being - with her men who had gone back to Blois to fetch larger ships.[4] For some of the troops and provisions had yet to arrive.

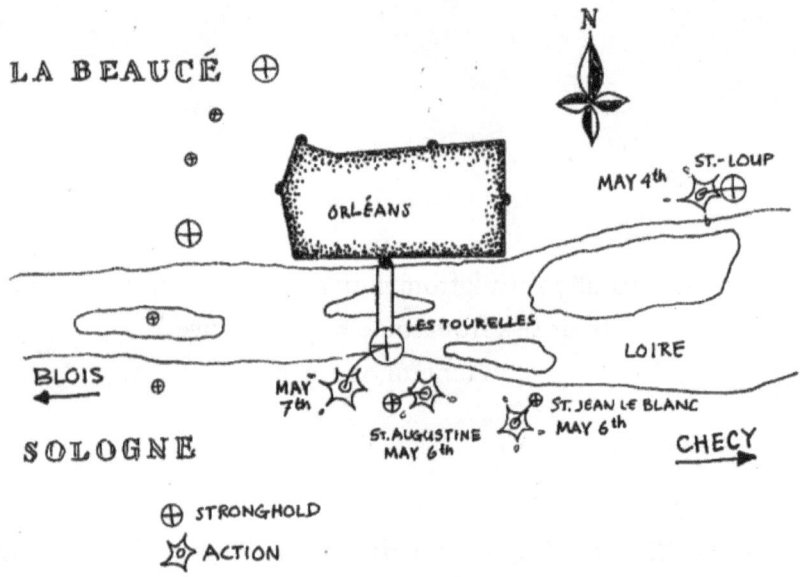

Siege of Orléans 1429

Saturday, 30 April, evening

Jeanne sends a herald to the English ordering them once again to leave and to release the herald whom she had sent from Blois with her first message; Jeanne's command is accompanied by a threat from the Bastard to kill English hostages.

Sunday, 1 May

Jeanne parades around on horseback, in full armour. The people are spellbound at the sight of her charismatic personality.[5] Then she speaks defiantly to the English from the bridge at Les Tourelles – a provocation she deems necessary now that the leadership of the French army appears so lethargic. Meanwhile, the Bastard goes to Blois to fetch additional troops. All the while, the Maid is engaged in the thorough assessment of the enemy positions.

Wednesday, 4 May

Jeanne rides with her co-commander La Hire at the head of a 500 men strong city militia towards the Bastard, who is returning from Blois with reinforcements.[6] The same day she withdraws to rest; meanwhile the city militia begins an impromptu storming of the bastion Saint Loup. The French are bloodily rebuffed. They seem to have erupted in cheer when Jeanne, awakened by her voices, shortly after appeared in the field, soon followed by the Bastard with his soldiers. Together with Jeanne, and with renewed enthusiasm, the bastion is taken within three hours (114 Englishmen are killed and forty imprisoned). This grim event constitutes Jeanne's first acquaintance with the atrocities of war and the sobering sight of dead and wounded people. Jeanne witnesses the violent and uncompromising attitude that is peculiar to people who are fighting for their lives. After this event, she wants soldiers to be publicly urged to go to confession before going into battle.

Thursday, 5 May, Ascension Day

Jeanne orders that this day there will be no fighting. She makes a last appeal to the English to leave. This third message is sent by arrow over the broken part of the bridge to Les Tourelles. The text reads as follows: 'The King of Heaven orders and commands you through me, Jeanne the Maid, to leave your fortresses and return to your country, and if you do not so I shall make an uproar that will be perpetually remembered.'[7] On this day, under the direction of the Bastard, a council of war takes place to which Jeanne is not invited.

Friday, 6 May

The French cross the Loire and occupy the abandoned fortress at Saint Jean-le-Blanc. The same day, the tower of the monastery Saint Augustine, reinforced by the English, is stormed. Only after capturing the tower is La Pucelle informed of the outcome of the preceding day's meeting that the fight would be stopped temporarily.[8] Jeanne explodes with anger; she believes that the momentum of this day should be exploited. The defense volunteers and many soldiers share her opinion. Jeanne scorns the decision and tells the messenger: 'You were in your counsel, and I in mine. And believe me that the counsel of my Lord shall be carried out while that of yours will be destroyed.'[9] Nevertheless, the Maid returns to the city after instructing her men to lay siege to the stronghold of Les Tourelles the same night.[10]

Saturday, 7 May

Jeanne leaves the city to join the civilian fighters out in the field (the knights stuck to the agreement between the commanders). With the help of the city militia, she opens the Porte de Bourgogne (which had to remain closed on the orders of the army captains). Jeanne thus moves ahead without blinking an eye. To Gaucourt, the governor of Orléans in charge of guarding the gate, she simply says: 'Whether you want to or not, the people will fight and occupy the bastion, whatever you have decided.' She goes on to attack the stronghold at Les Tourelles with her inspired warriors. Only now do the commanders give in to Jeanne's unstoppable urge to act. While storming Les Tourelles, her standard (depicting Christ) gives new hope at a moment of weakness. Jeanne is the first to put a ladder against the palisade fence of the bastion. As she has previously predicted, she is injured by an arrow that hits her between the neck and the shoulder.

Stephen Richey (2000) about this impressive moment: 'If there was a single event that clinched Joan's place as an admired equal member of the warrior elite of France, it was when she took an English arrow through her shoulder at Orléans – and after the arrow was pulled out, returned to the forefront of the fight with redoubled ardor. Hundreds of men saw her take that arrow and hundreds of men saw her come back, a bloodstain at her shoulder, her good arm waving her banner, her voice carrying over the din, shouting for one more assault. At that sublime moment she became forever their Maid and they became forever her soldiers. (...) Jeanne had what it took to make the haughtiest warrior nobleman accept and then admire her.'[11]

From the moment Jeanne returned to the battlefield, 'the English trembled with fear while the royal troops found their courage.'[12] The French, led by Jeanne, fought like lions. The struggle had already lasted most of the day and the Bastard had wanted to call off the attack. But the Maid stopped him and withdrew into a vineyard for prayer. On her return, she sat down by a ditch, gripping her standard with two hands. When the English saw her they were horrified while the French took heart.

During the final phase of the fight, Jeanne shouted to the commander of Les Tourelles, who was standing on a bridge between the fortress and the stronghold, 'Glasdale, Glasdale, surrender yourself, surrender to the King of Heaven. You have called me a whore. I have a lot of pity on your soul and with your people.' Suddenly the bridge collapsed and Glasdale fell – along with some of his troops – into the water where he drowned. [Later it turned out that the bridge had been undermined.] La Pucelle prayed for their souls.

Not long after, all the Englishmen in the fortress were killed or imprisoned. Jeanne returns to Orléans where she is received with joy. Her wound is treated and she eats four or five pieces of bread, dipped in wine and water, the only food she takes that day.[13] [NB. Capturing Les Tourelles, the French have shown exceptional courage.[14] This will be discussed in more detail further down.]

Sunday, 8 May

The Englishmen arrange themselves for battle, but Jeanne and Dunois do not fall into their trap. After all, it is precisely this defensive set-up, with archers on the flanks and knights in the second line, which has defeated the French again and again. La Pucelle prohibits an attack, partly because it is Sunday and the French are only permitted to *defend* themselves on the Lord's Day. After one hour, the English march away from the battlefield. Jeanne orders that the demoralised English are to be allowed to leave unhindered. The liberation of Orléans is a fact.

The clique around the king and his official apparatus – and possibly the king himself – have deliberately attempted to minimise the role of Jeanne d'Arc in the liberation of Orléans. This is evidenced by the rather neutral letter from the king to his subjects after he was informed of the deliverance of the city. Yet, almost everyone knew that the victory at Orléans was the work of Jeanne.[15] For example, see the observation of the then well-known Dominican Jean Nider: 'The miracles that she has performed are such that they do not only astonish France, but all the kingdoms of the Christian world.' In a letter to an unnamed prince, Alain Chartier, a French poet and political writer, compares her to Hector, Alexander, Hannibal and Caesar.[16]

'*O virgin singulière, Digne de toute gloire, the toutes praises, des honours divins, tu es la grandeur du royaume, tu es la lumière du lys, tu es la clarté, tu es la gloire, non seulement des Français, mais de tous les chrétiens.*'[17]

Additionally, I quote the ruling of the contemporary renowned French theologian Jean Gerson: 'The mission of Jeanne is to be regarded as a "bienfait divin"[18] in which an aspect of the natural order is added to the supernatural.'[19]

Gerson, Chartier and Nider were not Jeanne's only admirers. Countless commentaries appeared at the time. Venetian traders in Bruges, Germans in the vicinity of Basel, and Greeks in Constantinople were all fascinated by the wondrous deeds of La Pucelle.[20] Even Sylvius Piccolomini, the later Pope Pius II, was said to be delighted by the stories that reached him from France.[21]

Later on, Dunois stated that after the victory at Orléans he and others did not doubt the military skills of the Maid. After Orléans, he himself went with Jeanne to the king in Loches[22] to plead for offensive action. The heroine of Orléans specifically urged the king to conquer the Loire cities of Jargeau, Meung and Beaugency so that the road would be free to crown and anoint the king in Reims. But the king deliberates until the Maid begs him on her knees to forsake any further dallying and to go to Reims to be crowned as soon as possible.[23] Stephen Richey

(2000) writes the following: 'By taking this position, Jeanne demonstrated an intuitive but certain grasp of how things like politics, public symbolism, and military action need to be integrated into the formulation of a Grand Strategy... An illiterate 17-year-old peasant girl now dominated the national-political decisions of France. Jeanne's will triumphed over the undecisive Dauphin.'[24]

---

1. De Rais and Sainte-Sévère among others.
2. 'La Pucelle,' as Jeanne is now known everywhere, berates the Bastard of Orléans (the later Count Dunois) who had meanwhile arrived on the spot. [The Bastard of Orléans was in charge of the defence of Orléans.]
3. Curiously, the French carried all of this out without being attacked by the English.
4. See *Rehabilitation*, 06, p.2 of 9 of a downloaded file. Incidentally, the attack did not take place until the next evening. Jeanne stayed overnight in Chécy (Fabre, Dutch translation, p.129).
5. Jeanne did this because she was constantly visited by people who wanted to see her.
6. The Bastard, incidentally, entered Orléans via the East Gate, so by way of La Beauce (the right bank). He thus came along the shore that Jeanne had chosen to reach Orléans but which had been rejected by the commanders.
7. Roughly quoted on p.9 of 32 of a downloaded file in Richey (2000).
8. Awaiting more help from the king.
9. Quoted in Thomas (2000), p.285.
10. According to some, Jeanne had spent the night with her soldiers in front of the captured bastion.
11. Loosely translated.
12. Quoted in Richey (2000), p.5 of 32 of a downloaded file.
13. *Rehabilitation*, 06, p.3 of 9 of a downloaded file.
14. Cf. Roberts (2011).
15. Thomas (2000), p.299.
16. DeVries (2011), p.88.
17. 'O unique Virgin, worthy of all glory, all praise, all divine honour! You are the greatness of the kingdom, the light of the lily, the clarity, the glory, not only of the French, but of all Christians.'
18. 'Divine generosity.'
19. Quoted (and roughly translated) in Virion (1972), p.118. Jean Gerson was

Chancellor of the University of Paris before it came under English influence.
20. Thomas (2000), p.582.
21. Taylor (2010), p.50.
22. This is according to Pernoud & Clin (2011), p.85. Others believe that they went to Tours together (from where the king later left for Loches).
23. *Rehabilitation*, 06, p.4 of 9 of a downloaded file.
24. Richey (2000), p.11 of 32 of a downloaded file. In the original text this sentence is in the present tense.

3 THE LOIRE OFFENSIVE

'Act and God will act!'[1]
- Jeanne d'Arc

During the Loire offensive, the French successively stormed the English positions in Jargeau, Meung and Beaugency; subsequently they destroyed a large English army at the battle of Patay.[2]

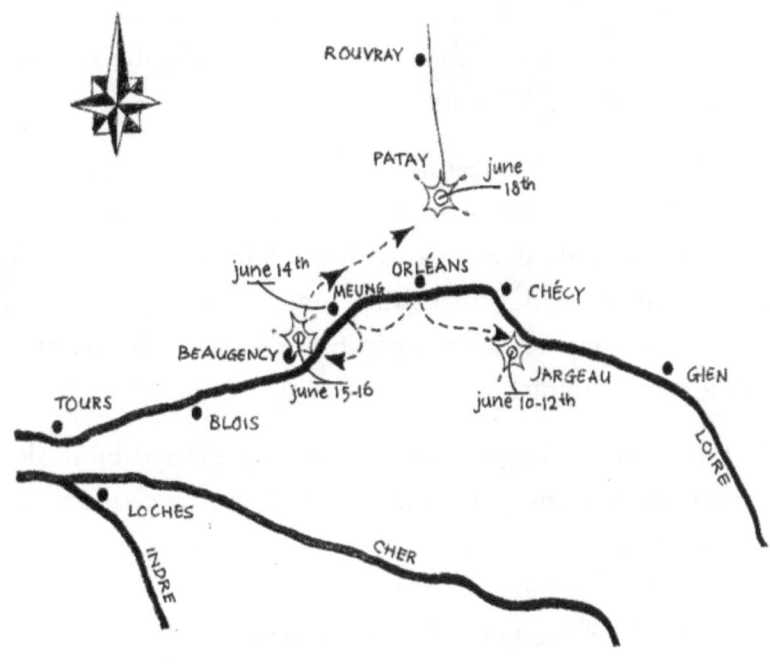

The cleansing of the Loire

Jargeau

Jeanne was part of the war council preceding the attack on Jargeau. In that meeting she confidently argued for a rapid attack, a vision which several commanders came to agree with. D'Alençon, the commander-in-chief of the Loire offensive, testified: 'When Jeanne saw that there were difficulties between [the commanders], she urged them not to fear any force majeure and not oppose an attack on the English because God was now in charge. She stated that if she had not been sure that God was in control, she would rather be herding sheep than expose herself to...dangers.'[3] The Duke of Alençon himself was not spared by our heroine. When she saw in him a trace of doubt about the speed with which she wanted to act, she said to him: 'Avant, gentil duc, à l'assaut!'[4]

On the battlefield, Jeanne's presence is again crucial. She appears at a critical moment with her inspiring white standard, a standard not only decorated with the lilies of the French kings, but dominated by Christ holding a globe. Facing Jargeau, she is the first to put a ladder against the wall of the town while passionately urging her men forward.[5]

In the battle for Jargeau, La Pucelle was praised by d'Alençon for her suggestions as to where to position the artillery. Jeanne also saves her 'gentil Duc' from death by asking him to leave a certain place, a spot that subsequently suffers the impact of a cannonball, killing a man. Jargeau falls on 12 June.

Meung

On 13 June, La Pucelle calls d'Alençon to her and shares with him her intention: 'Tomorrow after dinner I want to go to Meung. Make sure that the men are ready to leave at that time.'[6]

Meung falls almost without a blow on 14 June; the French army only had to fight to establish a bridgehead, which was quickly achieved. But what was the purpose of the manoeuvre? According to DeVries (2011), this task was undertaken so that English military activity could be blocked. By capturing the only accessible location to cross the Loire, Jeanne prevented a quick combination of the armies of Talbot and Scales with that of Fastolf when the latter would arrive on-site.[7] DeVries believes that it was an intelligent strategy 'which has not been given its weight in the study of Joan's campaigns.'[8]

Meanwhile, attracted by the success of Jeanne, more and more nobles and ordinary people join the army of the Dauphin.[9] Among those volunteers is constable[10] Arthur de Richemont (with his army), a high-ranking nobleman who had fallen out of favour with Charles VII by quarrelling with Georges de La Trémoïlle, the king's adviser. [As an aside, La Trémoïlle was through his father allied to the court of the Duke of Burgundy.][11]

For the Dauphin, the interference of Richemont is a very serious matter; he prohibits the captains of his army to allow the constable into the ranks, even though it has by now become clear that the English are approaching Patay with large reinforcements. DeVries (2011): '...no problem faced by Jeanne's army so far perhaps exceeded that created Richemont's approach. Because with the arrival of the constable on June 17th, a struggle for power between the leaders of the campaign threatens.'[12]

The Maid manages to persuade d'Alençon not to leave in protest. Later she would commit Richemont, who openly admired Jeanne's offensive strategy, to Beaugency. Jeanne's independent decision-making may have seriously harmed her relationship with the king. Some historians find herein an explanation for the fact that Charles VII failed to bail out Jeanne after her imprisonment by the English.[13]

Beaugency

While the French attack the city, Fastolf arrives with his army of about four to five thousand men. But the English commander, who would later become the model for Shakespeare's Sir John Falstaff, decides not to enter the fight and leaves quietly.

Richemont's presence may have been a factor in Falstolf's behavior. The constable was a battle-hardened man and his army of 1000 – 1200 men was a significant force. It was therefore a wise decision by Jeanne to accept the help of Richemont.[14]

In the end, Beaugency did not have to be stormed. A night of bombardment and the superiority in numbers of the French army was enough for the English garrison to surrender on 16 June.

The Battle of Patay

This battle takes place on 18 June when the pursuing French army encounters the retreating English led by Fastolf, Talbot and Scale.[15] The confrontation takes place in the open, just like Agincourt. [See Appendix II.] Jeanne's words at the meeting of the commanders of the French army prior to the battle have been preserved for posterity: 'In the name of God, let us fight them! If they were hung in the clouds, we would get them, for God sent them to us that we might punish them!...The gentle King shall have the greatest victory today that he has ever had. And my Counsel says to me that they are ours!'[16]

The battle ended in catastrophe for the English, partly due to a coincidence (a stag betrayed the presence of English archers in the bushes).[17]

The chronicler Jean de Wavrin, a loyal Burgundian embedded with the English army, attributes the victory of the French entirely to Jeanne d'Arc: 'She had gained such a name and fame that everyone believed that the enemies of King Charles could not put up any resistance, and the [French king] would soon be in possession of his entire kingdom.'[18]

The battle at Patay motivated the nobles to give the Maid more or less full command over the French army. In reality, Jeanne's role at Patay was limited because she was with the main body of the army. These units arrived late on the battlefield so that Jeanne could 'only' engage in mourning over the fallen, French and English alike.

The battle at Patay meant that several other cities surrendered to the French without a fight. For 'not only were there the promises of successful military support for the centers of population...but at the head of the military was a holy woman, a living saint, whose presence guaranteed divine justification for their decision to go against the English. Jeanne's reputation as a military 'savior' had travelled throughout occupied France and her mission was well known. She had promised to relieve the siege of Orléans, and she had; now she had promised to lead the king to Reims and his coronation; and no one in France, including the English, doubted that she would.'[19]

The growing defeatism of the English was described by the above-mentioned Jean de Wavrin: 'By the fame of Jeanne La Pucelle, the morale of the English got a nasty knock and they became very disheartened. They saw, it seemed to them, that lady Fortuna had turned against them, for they had already lost several cities and fortifications...mainly by the activities of La Pucelle...they saw that their people were defeated and that the usual thought and caution were lacking. They were, it seemed to them, very anxious to retreat to the region of Normandy and leave their former positions in France for what they were.'[20]

---

1. Or: 'God helps those who first help themselves.'
2. Richey (2000), p.11 of 32 of a downloaded file.
3. Quoted in Pernoud (1962), p.132 and roughly translated.
4. Quoted in Pernoud & Clin (2011), p 95. 'Forward, kind duke, charge!'
5. Richey (2000), p.5 of 32 of a downloaded file.
6. Quoted in Richey (2000), p.11 of 32 of a downloaded file; Thomas (2000), p.316.

7. John Talbot (Earl of Shrewsbury), Lord Thomas Scales and Sir John Fastolf were English captains.
8. DeVries (2011), p.103.
9. 'Throughout history soldiers have always followed a successful general.' Montgomery (1961), p.60.
10. A constable had the task of building the royal army – out of nothing in some cases, as armies were organised on an ad hoc basis at this time. To this end, the king had to raise taxes. [Only with Necker, state loans were introduced.] Personal communication Jules van Rooyen (2014). A constable was therefore a very important man
11. Incidentally, Richemont found La Trémoïlle too docile against the English.
12. DeVries (2011), p.103.
13. Cf. DeVries (2011), p.106.
14. DeVries (2011), p.108.
15. This battle probably took place near Saint Sigismond.
16. DeVries (2011), p.110.
17. The English suffered 2000 – 4000 deaths and 200 prisoners (on a total of 5000).
18. Thomas (2000), p.323. Freely translated.
19. DeVries (2011), p.118.
20. Quoted in Pernoud (1962), p.131. Roughly translated.

4 THE MARCH ON REIMS

'Loyaux Français, venez au-devant du roi Charles, et (...) ne vous doutez pour vos corps, ni vos biens, si ainsi faites; et si ainsi ne le faites, je vous promets et certifie sur vos vies que nos entrerons à l'aide de Dieu, en toutes les villes qui doivent être du saint royaume et y ferons bonne paix ferme, qui que vienne contre.'[1]
- Jeanne d' Arc

Eleven days after the Battle of Patay, the famous coronation tour to Reims begins (starting at Gien where the king resided). The campaign could not have started without pressure from Jeanne because the clique around the king was strongly opposed to her plan. However, the king gave in, for he saw with his own eyes that the army was fully devoted to the Maid.

On the way to Reims the army passes Auxerre. The city is not attacked because the city council has made a private arrangement with Philip the Good through La Trémoïlle (who earned a handsome amount of money in the process). Then the French reach Troyes. This fortified city initially wants to oppose

Charles VII, but is soon forced to support the king. [It should be noted that the French were in a more difficult situation than the besieged could possibly suspect; the army was struggling with supply issues causing a serious lack of provisions.]

At the gates of Troyes, Jeanne once more played a leading role. This siege may even be seen as her finest hour, for La Pucelle was the undisputed commander of the French army: it was the Maid who, in the question of whether the city should be besieged or not – over which the army commanders were divided – forced the breakthrough, this time against even larger opposition. 'Noble Dauphin,' she says, 'command your people to lay siege to the city of Troyes and no longer lose time with meetings. In God's name, even before three days are over, I will guide you into this city, by hook or by crook, and the false Burgundians will be stunted.' Before it even comes to a siege, Troyes capitulates (10 July) and the king makes his entrance 'en grande pompe' with Jeanne and her standard by his side.

When the army of Charles VII, animated by La Pucelle, moves to Reims it snowballs through the influx of volunteers, all attracted by the success, the spirit and the charisma of Jeanne. [Certainly not by the image of a weak and penniless king![2]]. 'Since the success at Troyes, which is to be traced back to Jeanne,' writes Heinz Thomas (2000), 'the campaign had been changed into a procession in which the people flowed together to crown the king and to honour the Maid sent by God who made this triumph possible.'[3]

There has been a lot of discussion about the march on Reims. According to Dunois, the royal advisers and army captains wanted to head to Normandy after the successes along the Loire. But the Maid, according to the Bastard, 'was invariably of the opinion that it was necessary to go to Reims to crown the king.

She surmised that once he was crowned and anointed, the power of his opponents would be continually diminish so that they could not disadvantage him, neither his person nor his kingdom.'[4]

Régine Pernoud ('eine der besten Kennerinnen von Jeanne's Geschichte')[5] is also of the opinion that all documents indicate that the decision to march to Reims to anoint the king, was pushed through by the Maid, in spite of the views of La Trémoïlle and Regnault de Chartres (archbishop of Reims and chancellor).[6] Once again, the Maid triumphed.

As the French approached Reims, the negotiations with the various cities on the way became shorter and shorter, the waiting became less difficult, and the army moved with more certainty.[7]

---

1. 'Loyal Frenchmen, choose the side of King Charles! And if you do, do not let yourself be carried away by guesses about the fate of your body and your goods; if you are not on our side, then I promise and assure you on your life that we will enter all the cities belonging to the Holy Kingdom with the help of God; we then will bring real peace; and all this will happen, whoever goes against us.' Very freely translated.
2. Now the army of the Dauphin had grown to approximately 12000 men. See also Taylor (2010), p.56.
3. Thomas (2000), p.361. Freely translated.
4. *Rehabilitation*, 06, p.4 of 9 of a downloaded file.
5. Thomas (2000), p.473.
6. Pernoud (1962).
7. Pernoud & Clin (2011), p.102.

5 THE CORONATION

*'Only a constant purpose can endow events
with stable meaning.'
- A Course in Miracles*

Approaching Reims, Jeanne has to talk sense into the king to reassure him. The king believes that there is too little artillery to overcome any opposition. The Maid predicts: 'Do not doubt, for the citizens of Reims will rush towards you.' And indeed, Reims welcomes the king on 17 July. The investiture – fully in line with Carolingian constitutional tradition and popular sentiment – takes place with Jeanne d'Arc in a prominent role. Through the coronation, demonstrating that the king rules by heavenly appointment, the existence and survival of an entire nation is ensured.[1] Jeanne is at the pinnacle of her power. With France restored as 'Beau Mystère,'[2] 'nothing, it seemed, could threaten her position.'[3]

The coronation took place on the morning of 17 July 1429 and lasted from nine o'clock in the morning to two o'clock in the afternoon. This phase of the mission of Jeanne d'Arc expressed that the king is the image of Christ.[4] Prior to the ceremony, the 26-year-old monarch was knighted by d'Alençon.

As part of the coronation, four knights were appointed to pick up the sacred oil for the anointing of the Frankish kings from the Abbey of Saint-Rémy.[5] After their return, the royal sword, covered with engraved French lilies, was brought in procession to the altar. The anointing (of chest, shoulders, elbows and wrists) through which Charles' body was consecrated for the service to God for the benefit of the people, was done through slits in the clothing.[6]

Charles, who wore shoes decorated with French lilies, then took the oath that he would honour justice and the law and defend the Church and the people (especially the poor and disadvantaged) against enemies. Thereafter, the king was led to the main altar where his head was anointed and a ring was put on his right index finger (as a symbol of the unity between the monarch and the people), accompanied by the words of the archbishop: 'O Christ, sacrez vous-même le roi pour le gouvernement comme vous avez sacré les prophètes, les rois, les martyrs.'[7]

To the sound of trumpets and the acclamations of the brilliantly dressed attendees, the crown was placed on Charles' head. [Six paladins of France, seconds before the actual coronation, held the crown above Charles VII's head.]

Then follow the tears of La Pucelle who embraces the king's legs and tells him that what she had been commanded by God has now become reality. Jeanne is deeply touched because in the coronation of Charles VII she sees a tangible sign of something that could establish the kingship of Christ deep in the souls of people.[8] Her presence, writes Donald Spoto (2007), must have made a profound impression on all those present (including her parents) because the coronation justified a woman who would normally have made a suspicious impression in the male world of the court, the army and the clergy.[9]

The Maid herself does not dwell on the ceremony. The same day, she dictates a letter to Philip the Good in which she exhorts him to establish peace with the king of France. She lets him know that the king and the duke must forgive each other, 'as Christians should', and that if the duke is hell-bent on fighting, he can do so against the Saracens. She finishes by saying that she will recommend him to God and that she will pray to God for peace.

Jules Eugène Lenepveu (1819-1898) painted a majestic mural depicting the coronation (Pantheon, Paris). Almost half of the painting is occupied by the nave of the cathedral, with two slender stained glass windows in the background. Various flags and banners accentuate the space. The mural shows the grand moment of Jeanne, the tallest figure (including her standard), a split-second away from the erupting triumphal cheer. The Maid of Orléans stands close to the king. She is in full armour and holds in her left hand her banner, the silent witness to so much struggle. In her right hand she holds her sword. While the king bows his head to receive the crown, Jeanne looks upwards, as if seeing something. Her key role in the unfolding event is clear.

Centuries after the resounding success of the journey to Reims, it remains mysterious why the Duke of Burgundy, nor Bedford, never made any attempt to prevent this solemn vesting of Charles VII with royal dignity (of which they knew the sacral effect).[10]

Following Jeanne's grandiose military successes and the coronation in the shadow of her illustrious standard, the later solemn consecration of the English king in Saint Denis as a competing act could only disappoint, in all respects.[11]

Meanwhile, Charles VII, now the anointed king of an enthused kingdom, weakens (!) the positions of the people who have brought him to the throne. It would have been a perfect moment to get through to Paris: the English and Burgundians were in chaos and the city was not defended.[12] Jeanne thinks of nothing but the immediate continuation of the campaign. But instead, the king *immobilises* his army and agrees a reprehensible armistice of 14 days with Philip of Burgundy for a promise (that is quickly broken) that Philip will surrender Paris. [The armistice had already been arranged before the coronation by Trémoïlle in consultation with the Burgundian court![13]]

Jeanne never believed Philip's promise. On 5 August, she dictates: 'I am not satisfied with a cease-fire and I do not know if I will keep to it. But if I do it, it will be for the good name of the king; one will no longer deceive the descendant of the royal house, for I will continue to lead the King's army and keep it together, to be ready after aforementioned fourteen days when they do not conclude peace.'

In the meantime, the Burgundian – with Bedford – is purely interested in playing for time; he deceives the king and gets away with it. The garrison of Paris is extended and the walls are strengthened. Jeanne and d'Alençon are powerless.

---

1. Virion (1972), p.215.
2. Virion (1972), p.229. Translates as 'beautiful mystery'.
3. DeVries (2011), p.128.
4. 'The king as image of Christ.' Virion (1972), p.213.

5. The use of the 'saint chrême' (from the sacred ampoule) was a privilege bestowed upon Reims by Popes Victor II and Urbanus II. Virion (1972), p.192.
6. Fabre (1948, Dutch translation), p.185.
7. Virion (1972), p.214. Translates as: 'O Christ, crown the king for governance as you have crowned the prophets, kings, and martyrs.'
8. Cf. Virion (1972), p.217.
9. Spoto (2007).
10. Warner (2000), p.70/71.
11. Virion (1972), p.193. The English king was not anointed with the saint chrême.
12. Richey (2000), p.13 van 32.
13. Pernoud & Clin (2011), p.115.

6 THE JOURNEY TO PARIS

"What...makes people unhappy is not too little choice, but too much," said Mitchell Layton. "Having to decide, always to decide, torn every which way all of the time."
- *The Fountainhead*, Ayn Rand

Typical of the trek to Paris is its long and winding course (Château-Thierry is passed twice). For outsiders, it was not clear whether this journey, which caused a loss of one and a half month, was the result of (a) strategic considerations, (b) unexpected manoeuvres of the enemy [to exhaust Charles' army], or (c) indecision on the behalf of the king and his counsel, partly as a result of the talks with Burgundy which had started on 21 August in Compiègne, without Jeanne's knowledge.

The aforementioned talks culminated in an armistice for the French to the north of the Seine, proclaimed on 28 September by Charles VII and only tacitly accepted by the Burgundians.

This 'abstinence from fighting' would be extended, thus giving the English and Burgundians ample opportunity to strengthen their relations and to prepare a spring offensive (including against the strategically located Compiègne).

Charles VII, after Reims, is thus kept dangling and led up the garden path. Charles himself admitted publicly on 6 May 1430[1] that he had been fooled.

Jeanne had never trusted the Burgundian.[2] The Maid of Orléans would therefore have preferred to forge ahead to Paris. Instead, her king's abeyance depresses her. A nervous atmosphere prevails in the army, and, against the will of Jeanne,[3] a 'drôle de bataille' took place at Montépilloy i.e. a battle that should have been a battle but was not (as nothing happened and the two armies returned home).

Immobilising the French army to create space to negotiate slowly but surely drains the faith in the victory that the Maid had instilled. Nothing is so disastrous for morale as indecision and doubt. Nevertheless, during the journey to Paris, more and more cities join the party of Valois, even cities that Charles VII had only passed through. But meanwhile, the discipline of the army deteriorated, an army that was also pulled apart 'as an octopus with its tentacles spread'[4] to guarantee the lasting subjugation of the many cities.

The campaign from Reims to Paris reflected that the French army was no longer led by the will of Jeanne d'Arc but by diplomats of the uncertain king and his counsel, primarily Trémoïlle.[5]

On 23 August 1429, the caravan with Jeanne and her co-fighters finally headed for Paris. The king's meandering route – according to Lucien Fabre (1948) – delayed the liberation of

France by a quarter of a century and led to the stake for the holy girl.⁶

Meanwhile, Archbishop Regnault de Chartres makes proposals to the Duke of Burgundy that would have outraged Jeanne.⁷ On 28 August 1429, a general armistice is quietly concluded in Compiègne. Paris initially fell outside its boundaries so Charles VII could have attacked the city, if desired. But because Philip the Good has now been offered to become governor of Paris by the English (Philip played both sides and Bedford wanted to mollify him) the Duke declares, *after* concluding the agreement, 'that he could not unite it with his honour to remain neutral when the king attacked Paris.'

Jeanne d'Arc and d'Alençon attacked Paris on 8 September, probably with permission from the king but without his active cooperation (on the contrary!).⁸ Their attack on Porte Saint-Honoré was possibly a diversion, or they might have wanted to seduce the Parisians into firing. Another possibility is that the French had wanted to bring about a revolt of the royalists in Paris. Jeanne, however, stated during her trial that she did want to take the canals and the walls.⁹

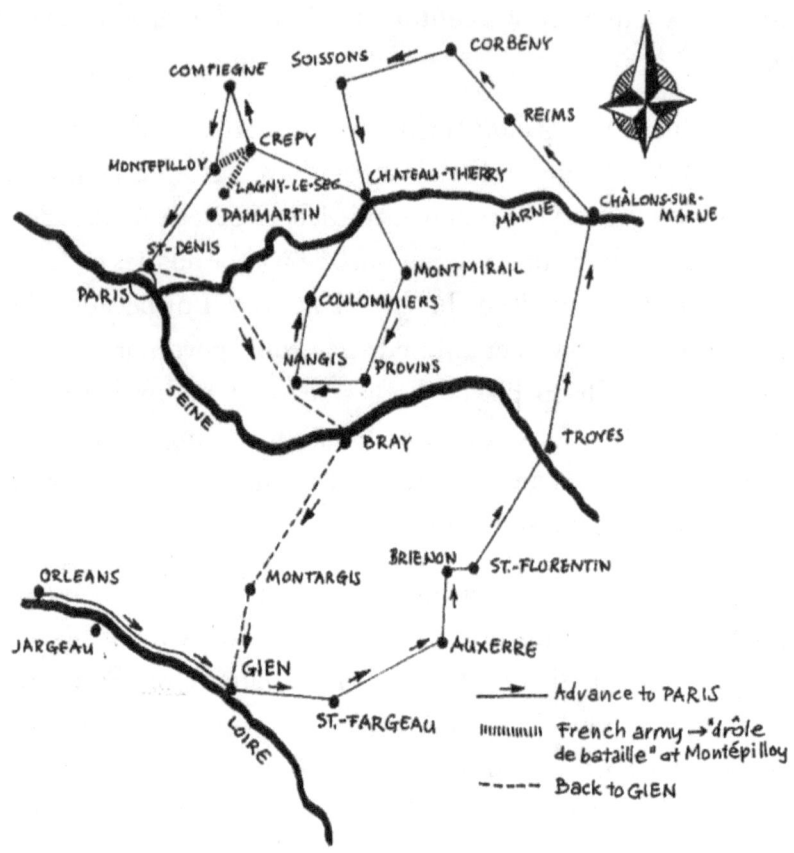

Jeanne d'Arc's journey to Paris

During the attack on Paris, our heroine is struck by an arrow in her thigh. She is carried away against her will. Trémoïlle immediately takes this opportunity to end the attack prematurely.[10] Jeanne later says, 'By my sword, we could have taken the city,' and she was right. The difficult part was that the inner canal around Paris was much deeper than expected.[11] The night-time would have made for an excellent opportunity to cross the moat and storm the walls the following day – a sensible idea, because no big city can be conquered in one day.

The morning after her injury, La Pucelle wants to resume fighting, but now the king asks her (after urgent advice from Trémoïlle) to cease, as he assesses military action to be desperate and dangerous.[12] He orders the Maid to join him in Saint Denis. Jeanne is very disappointed; she already had another route in mind (for which D'Alençon had by now built a bridge of boats over the Seine). [On the orders of the king this bridge is secretly broken down, an act that Stephen Richey (2000) calls 'treason'.[13]]

The king, manipulated by Trémoïlle, is now back in contact with Philip the Good to negotiate an extension of the truce. The king therefore does not deviate from his commitment to diplomacy. He even decides to return to the Loire. Charles still thinks he can obtain Paris without a struggle.

Our heroine is inconsolable. She brings her armour and a conquered sword as a votive gift to the church of Saint-Denis.[14] After she shatters her beloved sword of Fierbois (she used the flat of the sword to beat a prostitute following the army[15]), 'the same hurt, loneliness and despair clawed at her soul as that she had experienced on the night near the canal in front of the walls of Paris.'[16]

Against her will, Jeanne has to go to Gien on 21 September 1429.[17] The king then dissolves the French 'coronation army'. He sends d'Alençon, the most loyal ally of Jeanne, back home. [The two would never see each other again.] Subsequently, the king tries to reassure his nationals: he promises them 'if necessary,' i.e. if the Duke of Burgundy does not keep his promise, to return with 'une grande Armée' to complete the reconquest of his territories. But no one knows, of course, what those words are worth at that time. And Charles VII does not yet realise that he is being deceived.

It is certain that the Maid was not to blame for the failed attack on Paris. [Taylor (2010) in *The Virgin Warrior* is completely wrong.] A walled large city like Paris, which is defended by artillery, cannot be conquered in one night, not even with the most effective siege weapons. On the other hand, there is no moat so deep it can't be taken. And does not the old saying state that in some cases it is better to temporarily withdraw *pour mieux sauter*?

The attack[18] on Paris was blown off by the anti-Jeanne cabal. Jeanne believed the city could have been taken.[19] Whether or not led by Providence, the diplomats had won over Jeanne's military approach. She gets given less important tasks and sees her powers reduced while Trémoïlle's star is on the rise. The latter becomes by far the most important adviser of the king.

With the aim of side-lining Jeanne so that the diplomatic negotiations with the Burgundians will not be disturbed, Trémoïlle's peace proposals become increasingly generous. He does everything possible to move Philip the Good, an unreliable partner, towards neutrality. As a result, more and more cities north of the Seine fall into the hands of the Burgundians. Even Reims is threatened again at one point.[20] The same applies to other important cities, such as Compiègne. It is precisely to safeguard the strategically crucial, royalist Compiègne such a fate that Jeanne at a given moment, but now as an *independent* captain with three to four hundred non-French mercenaries, moves to the city.

As an independent 'captain', she has no influence over Charles

VII's strategy, but on the other hand, her *tactical* autonomy has greatly increased.[21] Unfortunately, her mercenary army cannot offer her the same loving loyalty as her former army, composed of Frenchmen. And for Jeanne stretches out 'the ever-darker road which would lead to imprisonment, torture and martyrdom.'[22]

During her stay in Compiègne, the city is encircled by Burgundian and English troops. The Maid can only make sallies. On one such occasion she is captured.

It is still a bone of contention between scholars whether or not she was betrayed by the commander of Compiègne (Flavy). Pernoud & Clin (2011) believe that the French saint sacrificed herself with a few others to save the city. Such things have happened before, for example during the outbreak at Korsoen-Kanev (1944) when two German infantry divisions sacrificed themselves to save the other units.[23] But Pernoud & Clin (2011) certainly do not exclude betrayal.[24]

---

1. Charles VII did this on the occasion of a declaration in which he proclaimed a general war against the Anglo-Burgundian alliance. Thomas (2000), p.504.
2. Jeanne told the king, 'You will find no peace, save at the lance's point,' a statement that is quite similar to the utterance that peace is only obtained through 'blood, sweat and tears'.
3. Thomas (2000), p.378.
4. Fabre (1948, Dutch translation), p.195.
5. Pernoud (1962), see also Thomas (2000), p.364.
6. Fabre (1948, Dutch translation), p.192.
7. The proposals 'undermine the political and military consequences of the coronation....' Fabre (1948, Dutch translation), p.193. See also DeVries (2011), p.140.
8. For the behaviour of the king, see below on the subject of the demolition of the bridge commissioned by D'Alençon. La Trémoïlle was against an attack on Paris anyway.

9. Thomas (2000), p.406) judges such an 'eigenständige Aktion' to be useless. [He evidently knows better than Jeanne!] 'Trotzdem setzte die Jungfrau ihren Angriffsversuch fort, bis ihre Verletzung und die hereinbrechende Nacht die Gefährten zur Einstellung ihrer Aktionen veranlassten.'
10. The actual order to withdraw from Paris (on 8 September) was given by Trémoïlle (who would put an end to the venture).
11. Apparently this was missed at the reconnaissance stage.
12. Cf. Thomas (2000), p.412/413.
13. Richey (2000), p.13 of 23 of a downloaded file.
14. Hobbins (2012), p.134.
15. Until the 18th century, camp followers were a normal phenomenon; many spouses (possibly even with their children) followed their husbands and carried out useful logistical tasks (carrying luggage, doing laundry, nursing the wounded).
16. Thomas (2000), roughly translated.
17. The voices of Jeanne had instructed her to remain in Saint Denis. Thomas (2000), p.432.
18. Newman (1942), p.21.
19. Quoted in Virion (1972), p.33.
20. The inhabitants of Reims felt compelled to write Jeanne a letter about this situation.
21. Richey (2000), p.13 of 32 of a downloaded file.
22. Ibid.
23. DeVries (2011), p.102.
24. Pernoud & Clin (2011), p.140.

7 JEANNE'S ATTRIBUTES

'Military genius is a gift of God, but the most essential quality of a general-in-chief is the strength of character and resolution to win at all costs.'
- Napoleon[1]

To understand the leadership of Jeanne d'Arc properly, the student must first of all have knowledge of her natural characteristics; for one is *born* a leader, even though the abundance of leadership courses suggests one could learn such a thing as well.

According to Lucien Fabre's research (1948), Jeanne had black hair and was blessed with a beautiful bosom. According to Jeanne's bodyguard (Jean d'Aulon), the Maid of Orléans was 'young, attractive and well-formed.'[2] And in more or less the same spirit speak other people who knew her. Perceval the Boulainvillers, chamberlain of Charles VII, describes her as follows: 'This Pucelle has a certain elegance; she has a masculine attitude, speaks little, and exhibits an admirable prudence when she speaks. She has the voice of a gracious woman and is very restrained in everything she eats and drinks; she likes riding horses, loves pretty weapons, and is very keen to be in the company of noble warriors. She abhors meetings and gatherings with many people, easily cries many tears, and has a cheerful face.'[3]

In short, the French national heroine must have been a feast for the eyes. But no matter how attractive she was, no soldier experienced any physical desire, or at least dared to express them in her presence. Under oath, Jean de Metz, a companion on her way to Chinon, declared that he never sexually coveted her. 'Jeanne,' admitted de Metz, 'fulfilled me of such a respect that for nothing in the world I had ever dared to molest her.'[4] De Metz's confession is confirmed by the then 36-year-old Bertrand de Poulengy, another travel companion of Jeanne on her journey to Chinon: 'I was young then, but I have never experienced any physical desire for her. I would have never dared to violate her by the great goodness I saw in her.'[5]

Compare the testimony of the knight Gobert Thibault: 'In the field she was always in the company of soldiers and [I] had heard many of Jeanne's intimates say that they never coveted her. That is to say, they sometimes had a sexual lust, but they never dared to heed them; they believed that it was impossible to desire her. And often, when they talked about the sins of the flesh, and used words that could provoke exciting thoughts, it was impossible for them to pursue the conversation when they saw her approaching, because suddenly their sexual feelings were gone.'[6] Corresponding declarations were made by D'Alençon and Dunois.

What our heroine did inspire was love, that of the purified, chaste kind. But more on that later.

It is striking that everyone who met Jeanne found her simple, honest, good, generous and 'divinely virtuous'. The Bastard of Orléans simply stated that Jeanne was sent by God.[7] *He experienced her behaviour in war as divine rather than human.*[8]

Those who accompanied Jeanne on the way to Chinon were full of praise. 'During eleven days of observation, they have not been able to detect any defect or weakness in her, but exemplary piety and Caritas and an unshakable determination.'[9] Pernoud and Clin talk about a 'pureté total du personnage.'[10] The scholars at Poitiers were also unable to find any detrimental qualities. 'In Jeanne,' they wrote, 'nothing bad is to be found, only **good**, **humility**, **virginity**, **devotion**, **honesty** and **simplicity**.'

The Maid was also not forceful [which, for example, is said of the famous German Field Marshal Rommel, to whom I will devote some lines below.[11]] Jeanne's modesty showed during her trial, when she said that she felt very uncomfortable with the adoration bestowed upon her. Mr. Pierre des Versailles (quoted by the parliamentarian Jean Barbin) reported that Jeanne told him that she trusted God to protect her from the dangers of idolatry.[12]

But in all her attractiveness and simplicity, the Maid of Orléans also easily inspired **awe**, yes, even **fear**. The Duke of Bedford implicitly admitted this when he was forced to carry out written orders to discipline English soldiers who deserted for fear of Jeanne's 'magic arts'. A somewhat similar fear can be identified in the followers of the French saint. The then thirty-year-old Jean de Metz, leader of Jeanne's escort to Chinon, who slept next to her at night [Jeanne laid herself to rest in full armour], said he was afraid of her.[13] When the Bastard of Orléans faced La

Pucelle, he immediately recognizes her ability to inspire awe (and later her divine mission).[14]

To further illustrate this quality, I would like to draw attention to the moment 'gentilhomme' Guy de Laval describes when Jeanne mounts her horse:

'I saw her mount her horse, all in white armour excepting the head, a little axe in her hand. The great black charger was very restive at her door and would not let her mount. 'Lead him,' she said, 'to the cross which is in front of the church,' and there she mounted, the horse standing still as if he had been bound.'[15]

It is clear that the writer of these words is full of admiration and awe.

One of the most striking features of the Maid of Orléans was her unshakable **self-confidence**. She was not in the least impressed by the nobility she encountered.[16] See, for example, the moment she meets the Bastard of Orléans for the first time in Chécy: 'Are you the Bastard of Orléans?,' asks Jeanne, only to immediately berate him for the bad counsel he gave her by claiming that it was better to approach Orléans along the (left) bank. 'In God's Name,' she said, 'the counsel of my Lord is safer and wiser than yours. You thought to deceive me, and it is yourselves who are deceived, for I bring you better succour than has ever come to any general or town whatsoever – the succour of the King of Heaven. This succour does not come from me, but from God Himself, Who, at the prayers of Saint Louis and Saint Charlemagne, has had compassion on the town of Orleans, and will not suffer the enemy to hold at the same time the Duke and his town!'[17] [The Duke was then a prisoner in England.]

Another illustration of Jeanne's self-confidence is the way in which she addresses the Bastard, before the hostilities at

Orléans, when she wants him to warn her if the English get reinforcements: 'Bastard, bastard, bastard, in the name of God, I command you that as soon as you know of the coming of Fastolf, you must let me know, because if he passes without me knowing, I promise that I will cut off your head.'[18] And then the words the girl from Domrémy uses to address the knight telling her on Friday 6 May (after the conquest of the siege tower of Saint Augustine) that the captains had decided that they were too few to fight for Les Tourelles: 'You were in your counsel,' says Jeanne, 'and I in mine. And believe me that the counsel of my Lord shall be carried out while that of yours will be destroyed.'

Jeanne, in short, treats the nobles and the mighty personages whom she meets as her equals, the king excepted. [Realise that she meets them with the shocking intention to admonish a foreign monarch, defeat his troops, conquer his fortresses and deprive him of his cities!]

Jeanne was **brave** from the outset. At the time of her stay in Vaucouleurs, she lectured the Duke of Lorraine, who thought she could work a miracle for him. Instead, the girl from Domrémy highlights his immoral (sexual) conduct and moreover asks him to make his son (René d'Anjou, brother-in-law of the Dauphin) available for her army (which he later did).[19]

La Pucelle was also the first to put a ladder against the bastion of Les Tourelles during the siege of Orléans.[20] Also at Saint Loup and Saint-Jean-le-Blanc she acted so boldly that even a man, schooled in war, could not have imitated her.[21] The captains openly wondered at her courage and perseverance.[22]

At the walls of Paris, La Pucelle showed no trace of fear during a rain of arrows and stones. She was always fully prepared to look the danger right in the eye. Read, for instance, the Bourguignon report by Georges Chastellain where he talks about Jeanne's arrest: 'The French, with their Pucelle, began to withdraw slowly...Seeing that, the Burgundians bravely attacked...and brought much damage to the French. Then La Pucelle – going beyond her feminine nature – made an extreme effort to safeguard her companions from defeat; she covered the retreat and was the bravest fighter in the whole company.'[23]

Based on her courage and ability, 'Frontschwein' La Hire considered the Maid his equal.[24] The famous fighter, always looking for trouble, was in Jeanne's back pocket. La Hire, without a doubt, followed the Maid, and not the other way around as Taylor wants us to believe.[25] Jeanne expressed herself to an old neighbour as follows: 'I fear nothing, except betrayal.'

Courage, self-confidence and charisma are great attributes. But Jeanne also had an exceptionally **strong will**, which could already be seen in Vaucouleurs where she told Braudicourt[26] that she wanted and had to go to the king, 'even if I have to wear down my feet to the knees.'[27] According to Richey, it was, in particular, her willpower that 'empowered her, a peasant girl, to browbeat royal officials into granting her an audience with the Dauphin – and, having won that audience, to persuade Charles to place her at the head of his army with a horse, a suit of armor, a sword, a banner, and an entourage of her own.'[28] Through mere willpower, she also successfully resisted Archbishop Regnault de Chartres, who wanted to halt the coronation tour at Troyes. Her entire life testifies to an unyielding will, such as has been rarely seen in history.

Adding to all that I have mentioned already, Jeanne was remarkably **healthy and full of life**. She was constantly in armour and barely ever slept. She was the opposite of the indifference and negligence that lost so many good opportunities in war. The Bastard of Orléans, the Duke of Alençon, the king and several others speak about her 'tireless urge to act'. The same thing can be said about Napoleon and Rommel (but not about Hitler after 1941). See the ruling of Clausewitz, the great theoretician of war: 'Whoever reads history without bias will not be able to evade the conviction, that of all the martial virtues the energy with which is fought has contributed most to glorious and successful achievements.'[29]

Jeanne was deeply **empathic** and **generous**: 'She always seemed to be genuinely committed to the suffering of her adversaries, and those whom she was called to help.'[30] Jean Pasquerel, the confessor of La Pucelle, highlights the following in this regard: 'I remember that on the night preceding the ascension of our Lord many Englishmen were killed. Jeanne wailed and said that they were killed without having been to confession. She cried over it and immediately came to me to confess; she asked me to publicly urge all soldiers to confess their sins and to thank God for the victory that had been obtained; if they did not, she would not stay with them but leave.'[31]

And here are Pasquerel's words about Jeanne's magnanimous behaviour on 7 May at the death of the English commander Lord Glasdale ('Classidas'): 'Jeanne was moved by pity and began to cry violently about the soul of Glasdale and the many others who drowned with him.' Louis de Coutes, Jeanne's page, also gave beautiful testimony about the empathy of La Pucelle: 'At one time, when the French carried away some English prisoners, one of the accompanying Frenchmen knocked one of them on the head and left him for dead. Jeanne, witness to the scene, rose from her horse, gave the Englishman the opportunity to confess, supported his head and comforted him with all her power.'[32] Supporting this story is Simon Beaucroix, a French écuyer ('Edelknecht') who served the Maid: 'She showed pity, not only to the French, but also to the enemy.'[33]

Should one be tempted to find the slightest trace of sentimentality in the empathy and the tearfulness of the heroic girl, then note the following: Jeanne believed that one cannot wage war with kid gloves. When her judges accused her of killing many Englishmen, she called it 'sweet talk' and added that the English only had to leave to be rid of all misery. Nothing in Jeanne's mind was sentimental, affected or ambiguous. On the contrary, she always kept a clear and logical head. [Many sins against the main principles of war were committed because all too often a good understanding of the situation was lacking![34]]

Because of her cool intelligence and rational mind[35], La Pucelle always acted deliberately. D'Alençon notes 'that she reacted prudently and mindfully' in matters of war. Jeanne's **prudence** was also mentioned by the theologians in their investigations of Jeanne in Poitiers. Jean Barbin remembers her carefulness: 'She replied very cautiously, as if she was a well-educated candidate notary; she did so in such a way that the learned men were amazed by her answers and believed that there was something divine, given her biography and her behaviour.'[36] Her prudence is also manifested in her military strategy. In the various letters she dictated, she sincerely offered her enemies peace (without sacrificing the prestige and rights of her homeland).[37] Her purpose was ultimately to avoid unnecessary struggle and in the case of Phillip of Burgundy she even begged and prayed for it.[38] All this shows great caution in the use of violence.

The Maid of Orléans could endure a lot of pain and had an **iron-strong constitution**. According to Perceval de Boulainvillers, she admirably handled 'the painful load of wearing a suit of armour' [think 35-40 kilos, probably more than her own weight]. At one point she has worn it for six days and six nights straight.'³⁹ Add to all this a lance weighing 6.5 kilos. Even the serious arrow wound she incurred at Orléans did not prevent her from quickly returning to the battlefield. Incidentally, the annals do not mention the *inflammation* that surely must have been the result of such a lesion. The same goes for the severe wound she incurred in front of the walls of Paris. The only thing we have is Jeanne's statement that it took five days before the wound in her thigh was healed [which did not prevent her from going to work the morning after!]⁴⁰

*In this context, we have an interesting analogy with Rommel, the respected German field marshal who played an important role in the war in North Africa during World War II. This esteemed warrior (Rommel 'was a soldier and warfare was his profession') was also injured. But unlike the Maid, he was eliminated by that injury (to his arm).*⁴¹ *The day after, Rommel had a high fever and talked nonsense, so he had to transfer the command to a colleague.*

The injury to the arm that Rommel suffered at the Carpathian front turned out rather badly. Rommel: 'I was weakened by blood loss and the stiff-tied arm and overcoat that was thrown around my shoulders obstructed me in my movements. I thought about giving up the command, but the difficult position of the detachment made me decide to stay in my post.'⁴² Compare the testimony of Dunois about the injured Jeanne at Les Tourelles: 'Jeanne was hit by an arrow that penetrated her body 15 cm at a place between her neck and shoulder. Nevertheless, she did not evade her military obligations and did not let herself be medically treated...I was about to suspend the fight and was already planning to bring the army back to the city. At that time the Maid came to me and asked me to wait. Thereupon she mounted her horse and pulled herself back into a vineyard at some distance *from the hustle and bustle; in that vineyard she remained in prayer for about eight minutes. When she came back, she immediately picked up her standard and took position on the edge of the ditch. From the moment she was there, the English trembled with terror.'*[43]

It was the resilience of La Pucelle that led to a turning point in the struggle for Les Tourelles!

Did 'the daughter of God' (as she was called by her voices) possess only a good sense of intuition or did she possess the **gift of prophecy**? Whatever its mysterious nature, the fact is that Jeanne predicted that the siege of Orléans would be lifted within five days. And this is what surely would have happened had she not been opposed. Moreover, in the same prophetic manner, she saved her 'gentil Duc' from a certain death. D'Alençon tells how Jeanne – at Jargeau – warned him to leave a certain spot, where a moment later a warrior was killed by a cannonball.[44] During the Loire offensive, prior to the Battle of Patay, d'Alençon asked Jeanne, in the presence of Richemont, the Bastard of Orléans and others, whether or not they should turn their back on the English. Jeanne replied: 'Oh no, the English will not defend and be overcome; and you will need spurs to chase them...It will be the greatest victory ever achieved for the noble king today. And my counsel has told me, we will get them all.' See also especially her statement when she arrived in Chinon: 'Je durerai un an, guère plus.'[45] That year, according to Jeanne, had to be well spent.

All four prophecies of Jeanne d'Arc as related to the king came true. The Maid freed Orléans and crowned the king. Furthermore, the Duke of Orléans was released and Paris – and later the whole of France – was freed from the English.

Was Jeanne a **genius**, on the same footing as Mozart? The answer must be affirmative, because no one can explain how she obtained her tactical and strategic knowledge. It has been said that Jeanne was 'expérimentée sans expérience'. If so, she must undoubtedly have had an *internal* knowledge that enabled her, an illiterate teen from the country, to deal as an equal with noblemen, clerical bookworms and high-ranking soldiers.[46] Jeanne herself was *not* aware of her knowledge. This is evident from her response to the voices that told her to go to Baudricourt. She replied that she was 'a poor girl who could not ride a horse and knew nothing of warfare.'[47]

It is said that although Jeanne knew a great deal about strategic matters, she was nevertheless quite ignorant. However, this 'communis opinio' may need to be questioned. Her confessor Pasquerel, who knew her well, certainly thought differently. And Loyseleur, a clergyman who played a treacherous role in the process against Jeanne, found her simple *but also very clever*.[48] She conversed in an astonishingly educated manner with the theologians in both Poitiers and Rouen.

Intelligence and perceptiveness were also characteristic of the French heroine during her battles. When soldiers under the great stress of combat fall back on experience or training, Jeanne always had a *clear mind* and acted authoritatively despite her lack of experience. Once the Maid of Orléans had made a decision, she stood firm. She did not shy away from risk. For instance, the journey to Reims through the enemy's heartland was certainly risky but by no means reckless.

The description of Jeanne is of a disciplined, fervent, pious girl[49] *with a fixed, practical and clear purpose. A virtuous, transparent and powerful type that – according to some – was to be regarded as a gift from God*[50]; *an angelic creature that by her nature encouraged and inspired anyone who needed it, for instance, during her journey from Vaucouleurs to Chinon; and in case of the ever-wavering Charles VII, scholarly theologians (who examined Jeanne's purity of intent in Poitiers) came to a similar judgement. They even declared that doubting Jeanne was a rejection of the Holy Spirit and made the sceptic unworthy of receiving divine help.*[51]

---

1. Quoted in Connelly (2002), p.13.
2. DeVries (2011), p.3. Jeanne d'Arc must have been around 1.60 m, Fabre (1948, Dutch translation), p.116.
3. Pernoud (1962), p.114. Roughly translated.
4. Rehabilitation, 04, p.2 of 5 of a downloaded file.
5. Rehabilitation, 04, p. 4 of 5 of a downloaded file.
6. Quoted in DeVries (2011), p.31.
7. Rehabilitation, 06, p.1 of 9 of a downloaded file.
8. Ibid.
9. See Pernoud & Clin (2011) in *Jeanne d'Arc*, their instant-classic reference work.
10. Pernoud & Clin (2011), p.58. It translates as 'a person of complete purity'.
11. Rommel wrote the book *Infanterie greift an*, a record of his experiences in the First World War. The book was used at European military academies as a textbook in military tactics. Rommel (2008), p.56.
12. Richey, (2000), p.6 of 32 of a downloaded file.
13. Thomas (2000), p.179.
14. Pernoud & Clin (2011), p.25.
15. http://www.maidofheaven.com/joanofarc_guy_de_laval.asp, accessed 2 October 2019.
16. The same is true for the chancellors, army commanders and favourites of the king that she met.
17. Quoted in Fabre (1948, Dutch translation), p.128; Thomas (2000), p.261, DeVries (2011), p.70. For the original, see Rehabilitation 06, p.2 of 9 of a downloaded file.
18. Pernoud (1962), p.99.
19. Pernoud & Clin (2011), p.33.
20. See Pernoud (1962), p.108.
21. Rehabilitation, 06, p.7 of 9 of a downloaded file (Thibauld d'Armagnac, knight).
22. Ibid.

23. Quoted in Pernoud (1962), p.178. Freely translated.
24. Thomas (2000), p.241.
25. Taylor (2010), p.82/83.
26. Henri Le Royer. http://www.stejeannedarc.net/rehabilitation/dep_henri_royer.php, accessed 23 January 2020.
27. Rehabilitation, 04, p.3 of 5 of a downloaded file.
28. Richey (2000), p. 14 van 32 of a downloaded file.
29. Clausewitz (1987).
30. DeVries (2011), p.93.
31. Pernoud (1962), p.99. Freely translated.
32. Pernoud (1962), p.71.
33. Ibid.
34. Mantel (1931), p.127.
35. Thomas (2000), p.583.
36. Quoted in Pernoud & Clin (2011), p.51. Roughly translated.
37. Virion (1972), p.70.
38. See her letter to Philip of Burgundy of 17 July, 1429.
39. Pernoud (1962), p.114.
40. In this context, it is also worth mentioning that during an attempt to escape her imprisonment in Beaurevoir, Jeanne jumped out of a tower room 22 metres from the ground, a leap that she miraculously survived.
41. Rommel wrote: 'I got little sleep that night because my wound was hurting and my nerves were tense by the battles of the last day – not to mention the care I had for the work of the following day.'
42. Sibley & Fry (2008), p.35.
43. Quoted in Warner (2000), p.110.
44. Pernoud (1962), p.133.
45. Quoted in Pernoud (1962), p.166.
46. Richey (2000), p.14.
47. Hobbins (2012), p.73.
48. Taylor (2010). Prior to the process, Loyseleur visited Jeanne in her dungeon. He pretended to be a compatriot and a follower of Charles VII. In this way he deceived Jeanne in order to seduce her into statements that could be used against her. See Fabre (1948, Dutch translation), p.244. See also Thomas (2000), p.529.
49. Jeanne confessed almost daily and often received communion. Virion (1972), p.240.
50. Rehabilitation, 01, p.2 of 5 of a downloaded file.
51. Freely cited, Virion (1972), p.117.

8 JEANNE'S GENERAL SKILLS

'Skills are about the correct execution of certain (technical) acts and the practical introduction of the knowledge that has already been acquired.'
- Quote from a dictionary[1]

Jeanne acted with words. She always expressed herself clearly. No word left her lips that was not constructive or exemplary.[2] She had, in short, a talent for speaking. It made her effective and confident, both in dealing with nobles and communicating with her subordinates, an indispensable skill for a commander.[3] Jeanne could also formulate exactly and powerfully what was to be done on the battlefield, especially during difficult moments. It must have been wonderful to hear her speak.[4]

This is how she greeted the king that first time: 'Noble Dauphin, my name is Jeanne la Pucelle; I am sent by God to bring you and the kingdom help. And by me the Lord of Heaven lets you know, that you shall be anointed and crowned in Reims, and that you shall be the lieutenant of the King in Heaven, who is king of

France.'[5] A clearer, more effective summary of her mission is not conceivable. And here is how she, now housed in the castle of the king, greeted the Duke of Alençon (who had been curious of Jeanne): 'Vous soyez le très bien venu[6], the more French royal blood is gathered, the better.'

World-famous are her decisive answers during the investigation in Poitiers and the interrogations in Rouen (which fall outside the scope of this work). In general, one can say, Jeanne's answers are so sharply phrased, so clear, and so disarming that they made a profound impression on everyone, much more so than the miracles that an emerging legend already attributed to her.[7]

La Pucelle must also have been very **socially skilled**, a quality inseparable from her natural charm. She was liked wherever she went, people admired her. D'Alençon, for example, was delighted by her from the outset, if only because she – with a 'light-hearted boldness'[8] – addressed him on a first-name basis and playfully called him 'gentil duc' and 'mon beau duc'. The knight Gobert Thibault, to name another witness, testified that Jeanne, when he first met her, tapped him on the shoulder and said that she sure would like to have a few men of his type in her entourage.[9] Jeanne was thus generally admired. Lucien Fabre[10] wrote: 'Many citizens, councilmen, presidents of chambers of directors and notables in other areas went to visit her. Before meeting her, they were sceptically inclined, but afterwards they were all convinced. Not one was there, who doubted whether she had been sent by God. Often, they could not...stop crying, so friendly and charming was she when they talked to her.'

One should not forget that Jeanne, a simple, illiterate farmer's daughter, had access to the king and conversed with many other noblemen. The ease and effectiveness with which she interacted with these top figures is astonishing. See, for example, her dealings with Arthur de Richemont when he appeared at Beaugency. The constable was persona non grata; no one was waiting for him because no one wanted to affront the king (see Chapter 3).

When Richemont unexpectedly shows up at Beaugency, Jeanne welcomes him with the following disarming words: 'Fair constable, you are not on my wish here, but now you are here, I say to you a hearty welcome.' [Because she could use him and his troops very well!] Moreover, she managed to persuade d'Alençon and the other army commanders not to leave in protest, which would not have been strange given Richemont's excommunication. Jeanne was therefore clearly able to manage relationships, including her relationship with the king, whom she had to win over again and again.

Regarding the social skills of Jeanne d'Arc, the letter of 'gentilhomme' Guy de Laval (dated 8 June 1429) speaks volumes.[11] In this letter, Guy confesses to his grandmother, Anna de Laval, the widow of Duguesclin, one of the great patriotic warriors of France (for which Jeanne had much admiration), that he was hopelessly touched by Jeanne's radiance. And that he, with his brother, has signed up to serve Jeanne in the royal army. Guy writes: 'I went to her lodging to see her: and she sent for wine and told me we should soon drink wine in Paris. And there seemed something wholly divine in her manner, and in seeing her and hearing her.'[12]

Elsewhere he writes: 'The Maid told me in her lodging that she had sent you, grandmother, a small gold ring, which was indeed a very small affair, and that she would fain have sent you something better, considering your recommendation.'[13] In other words: Jeanne was socially skilful and was able to maintain relationships with high-ranking persons (such as Guy de Laval's great-mother). But the Maid could not only deal with individuals, she was also successful in dealing with 'royal councils' and 'boards' of cities like Reims, Tournai, and Riom. In short, the Maid was not an unworldly mystic.[14] She had charm, common sense, could network, was a winner, and combined this with a rare power and courage. It was this set of characteristics and abilities that made hardened soldiers adore her and at the same time instilled in them a sacred respect for her.

I should state explicitly that Jeanne was overwhelmingly **credible and convincing**. Several factors contributed to this. First of all, the values (and beliefs, attitudes, concerns and lifestyles) of her followers were similar to her own. Jeanne appealed to an existential need (in this case: security – because there were plenty of looting Englishmen around). And yes, Jeanne spoke clearly and concisely, formulated concrete goals (and took action) and was the right figure at the right time in the right place. Hence it is not surprising that she achieved resounding results (which added to her fame). *But the deepest source of her credibility and the emotions she inspired as well as the acclaim she received from all walks of life was that people saw Jeanne as a saint. Even the hostile University of Paris had to reluctantly admit that the country abounded with faithful warriors who joined Jeanne whose name went from city to city, accompanied by a reputation of holiness.*[15]

---

1. http://www.competentindesocialprofit.be/wat-zijn-competenties. Accessed 13 February 2020.
2. De Gaucourt, Rehabilitation, o5, p.2 of 9 of a downloaded file.
3. Cf. Liddell Hart (1944), p.222.
4. See Jean Maçon, a famous scholar in civil and canonical law,

Rehabilitation, 06, p.6 of 9 of a downloaded file. [Maçon is quoted by Cosma de Commy, Orléans town dweller.]
5. According to Raoul de Gaucourt, the governor of Orléans, these were the words that Jeanne used. See Fabre (1948, Dutch translation), p.98. About the word 'Lieutenant': Jeanne, in using this term, expresses her understanding of the essence of the feudal contract. She considers France to be a loan to the king, a loan to establish in France the Kingship of Christ. Thus, Charles VII in Jeanne's eyes is only a regent, a regent for God. Therefore, she could ask the king to give his kingdom to God so that God could then give it back to the king as a loan. However, Jeanne believes not only in the king as a representative of God, she also believes in the sanctity of blood and dynasticism. She is a forerunner of royal 'absolutism' ('King by the Grace of God'). It should be noted that the most absolute king, Louis XVI, still adhered to a legal system including a description of his prerogatives ('le système louisquatorzien'). Moreover, the Sun King respected the traditional freedoms and conventions, partly due to the existence of a culture of a Church with independent authority. See Hamburg (2012).
6. 'Be very welcome.' Fabre (1948, Dutch translation), p.103.
7. Fabre (1948, Dutch translation, slightly adapted), p.118.
8. Richey (2000), p.19 of 32 of a downloaded file.
9. Quoted in Richey (2000), p.19 of 32 of a downloaded file.
10. Fabre (1948, Dutch translation), p.106. Also: Jeanne always had good relations with her family, even though the contrary is often claimed. See Pernoud (1962), p.148.
11. Quoted in Pernoud (1962), p.130.
12. http://www.maidofheaven.com/joanofarc_guy_de_laval.asp, accessed 2 June 2014. Very freely translated.
13. Pernoud (1962), p.131.
14. Cf. Richey (2000), p.19 of 32 of a downloaded file.
15. Virion (1972), p.120.

9 JEANNE'S MILITARY SKILLS

'Endurance is not just the ability to bear a hard thing,
but to turn it into glory.'
- William Barclay

Jeanne d'Arc was a soldier. She was not a religious mascot who merely served as a moral compass. She bore arms, obtained the rank of commander and had armed men at her disposal (a 'bataille' – several units of 12-14 horsemen)[1] [2]. La Pucelle was a good soldier.

Q. What makes someone a good soldier?

Napoleon: 'The main characteristic that a soldier must possess is that he must be able to sustain and...[endure] fatigue and hardship [and in the meanwhile carry out his assignments]. Courage only comes second place.'[3]

Clausewitz, on the other hand, took a different view. Because danger is inherent to war, the foremost quality of good a warrior is – in Clausewitz' opinion – courage, both physical and moral. Jeanne was tireless *and* brave! During the long campaigns, she sleeps, like a common soldier, in the hay, without complaining. Stephen Richey (2000) writes: 'Throughout her military career, Joan displayed amazing stamina in wearing a heavy suit of armor and keeping the saddle all day, day after day, sometimes even sleeping through the night in her armor.'[4]

Jeanne was also a commander. She was a leader not only by nature, but formally appointed. After all, the king had proclaimed that 'nothing should be done without reference to the Maid, no matter how many good and competent men of war there may be present.'[5] Jeanne received, in addition to equipment, and in accordance with her status, certain privileges such as being allowed to carry a standard and being assigned squires and messengers. As I mentioned before: only high-ranking people were given an 'entourage'.

Moreover, after Jargeau, Jeanne was held in the same esteem as other captains (La Hire and de Xaintrailles for example) thanks to her decision-making and actions. However, official leader – say 'supreme commander' – she was not. At Orléans, the Bastard of Orléans was the supreme commander.[6] During the Loire campaign the Duke of Alençon was in charge, assisted by Marshal Sainte-Sévère and his future colleague Gilles de Rais (who would later become notorious as 'Bluebeard').[7] The 'gentil duke', as our heroine called d'Alençon, was fully devoted to the Maid by this time. He firmly believed that she was sent by God and allowed her to make all the strategic decisions,[8] at least at Troyes. It should be noted that not being the supreme commander was the reason La Pucelle could fight on the front lines.

Jeanne was an excellent rider, even with lance in hand. The latter was not a sinecure because a medieval lance, due to its weight and length, asked a lot from the shoulder muscles. D'Alençon, who saw her exercise when they first met, was impressed by her performance and gave her a horse out of admiration. Her equestrian skills are confirmed by the words of Marguerite la Touroulde, the wife of the financial adviser to the king and Lady of the Queen[9]: 'I have seen her ride a horse and wield a lance as well as the finest soldier, and the soldiers themselves were most astonished by this.'[10] The fact that Jeanne was an excellent rider had great significance as the core of the medieval army was formed by the cavalry. And when the knights were deployed, the lance was their most important weapon. Finally, if we call – in the footsteps of Field Marshal Montgomery – simplicity, decision-making and action military genius, then Jeanne d'Arc was a military genius.[11]

---

1. See De Vos (2006), p.125.
2. See Pernoud (1962), p.74.
3. See Sibley & Fry (2008), p.32 where Napoleon is quoted
4. Richey (2000), p.17/18 of 32 of a downloaded file.
5. Faber (1948, Dutch translation), p.123.
6. Pernoud (1962), p.90.
7. Engelstad (1988).
8. DeVries (2011), p.97.
9. Pernoud (1962), p.71,127; Thomas (2000), p.430.
10. Richey (2000), p.17 of 32 of a downloaded file.
11. Montgomery (1961), p.67.

10 THE FOLLOWERS OF LA PUCELLE

'Ihrer religiösen Sendung hat Jeanne vor allem auf ihren Bannern für jedermann sichtbar Ausdruck verliehen.'[1]
- Heinz Thomas

At the time of Jeanne d'Arc, most people were deeply religious, even though Christian unity was increasingly threatened by rebellion and heresy.[2] One can cite Wycliffe, Hus, Averroes, nominalism, the clerical opposition to the pope,[3] and the rebellions in Flanders;[4] but here the princes of Europe's increasing disregard for the authority of the Church is most relevant. It should also be remembered that the religious and moral decadence of the Renaissance could already be felt in certain circles. In short, the supranational building of the Church began to crack in the calamitous 14th century.

In this context, Jeanne d'Arc should be seen as (a) the *antithesis* of the revolutionary and subversive climate among intellectuals,[5]

(b) a fighter for the preservation of 'sacrality' in public life, (c) the defender of throne and altar, and – above all – (d) the promoter of the idea of the king as 'lieutenant du Christ au royaume de France'.[6]

Yet, the Church expanded and Catholics still believed in miracles. Jeanne's orthodoxy, sincerity and manifest relationship with God, solemnly affirmed by her successes, must therefore have contributed immensely to her power of persuasion. With her powerful religious rhetoric, which appealed to people's emotions, she built on what her cohorts already wanted to believe, i.e. that her authority was sanctioned by God. Even the members of the war council who were lacking in faith must have known that the key to morale was soldiers blindly trusting 'La fille de Dieu'. Time and time again she appealed to religion to get her nominal superiors to go along with her ideas.[7] The troubled times France was experiencing made her message more potent. At the altars, people everywhere lamented 'La grand pitié en France'.[8] And the roads to the pilgrimage site of Notre-Dame du Puy were busier than ever.

The followers of Jeanne d'Arc were pious, traditional Catholics who were loyal to the pope. They were people, therefore, who still believed in sacred values and norms and who were convinced that Jeanne was sent by God.

As mentioned, Jeanne inspired worship and enthusiasm from the outset.[9] After Orléans, the adoration reached a crescendo. The *Journal du Siege* paints a picture of nothing less than Jeanne-mania ('It was for the people as if God had descended in their midst').[10] During the process of rehabilitation Jean Barbin quoted a certain Mr. Pierre de Versailles; the latter had said that on the occasion of Jeanne's visit to Loches, 'the people grabbed the legs of her horse and kissed Jeanne's hands and feet'. And the aforementioned Marguerite La Touroulde testified that when the girl was a guest in her home, 'women came along with devotional objects that she had to touch'.

This overwhelming response[11] can be traced back to (1) the phenomenon of social contamination (people feeding off each other's emotions), and (2) the current French predicament that seemed to call for a saviour. In addition, there was above all the confidence in her mere presence and her clear 'divine virtue'.[12]

Among the English, however, Jeanne generated fear. That was the case, for example, on Saturday, 7 May (at Orléans) when she was injured by an arrow. By appearing at the front [the Bastard of Orléans wanted to withdraw] Jeanne instilled fear in the English and gave the French renewed courage.[13] The dawdling of Fastolf can thus be explained. He seems to have been demoralised and defeatist even before coming face to face with Jeanne d'Arc.[14] When he finally appeared at the Loire, he was reluctant (a) to give support to the English at Beaugency or Meung, and (b) to face the French himself.[15] When he finally fought at Patay, it was only because there was no alternative as the French attacked Fastolf during his retreat.[16]

***

Q. Was the 'Jeanne-mania' artificial?

A. Rumours about the Maid's journey to the king, according to Heinz Thomas (2000), did not reach Orléans organically, but were deliberately brought to the city.[17] The author of *Jeanne d'Arc, Jungfrau und Tochter Gottes* believes that Colet de Vienne, the messenger of the king, brought messages of that kind to Orléans.[18] Emilie Roberts (2011) posits that Jeanne consciously contributed to her own myth through her *Letter to the English*.[19] This was not because she wanted to deceive, but to convince potential warriors of her sacred mission.[20]

Taylor (2010) goes further and suggests that Jeanne d'Arc was *positioned* as a heroine by the mother-in-law of Charles VII (Yolanda of Aragon), in collaboration with the Dauphin himself. There is no evidence for this hypothesis. Pernoud & Clin (2011) make no mention of this theory whatsoever. Nevertheless, it is certain that the Bastard of Orléans had heard rumours 'that a certain young woman, whom one called the Maid, claimed that she would go to the noble Dauphin with help from heaven, break the siege of Orléans, and bring the Dauphin to Reims'.[21] Dunois, in order to clarify these rumours, sent two investigators to the king.[22]

If Jeanne was indeed *marketed*, one is reminded of the tactics employed prior to the arrival of the Beatles in America. But that such organised action was taken in the case of Jeanne d'Arc is, again, unproven. Yet, there must have been some tidings about Jeanne's performance because news reached the English. Jeanne's letter must therefore be reviewed in this light. It was a document that made official what was already a rumour, that the Maid who would save France had arrived and that her first goal was to liberate Orléans. She would cease only when the true heir to the throne, Charles VII, made his entry into Paris. 'This now would be the 'tumult' that was greater than any in the next thousand years. And it would start in Orléans.'[23]

There is some controversy regarding whether the mission of the Maid finished with the coronation in Reims, or whether her divine task also included the liberation of Paris. In either case, it is certain that Jeanne, while kneeling at the coronation of Charles VII – embracing his legs and shedding tears – spoke the following words for all to hear: 'Noble king, now the will of God is accomplished who desired that I would break the siege of Orléans and bring you to Reims to be crowned and anointed as a sign that you are the true king to whom the kingdom belongs.'

This statement sounds a lot like a formal conclusion to the military phase of her mission. [One could consider that in martial history it has seldom been possible to take the capital of an enemy.²⁴] It seems to me that if the taking of Paris would have been part of Jeanne's military mission – simply because the city is the heart of the mystical body of France – God would certainly have made this possible. It is therefore more reasonable to believe that the coronation in Reims completed the first part of her mission, and that the second part consisted of a *martyrdom* that would etch the image of Jeanne d'Arc deep into the collective memory of humanity.²⁵ This would be another kind of victory for Jeanne. Doubt about the boundaries of her mission exists only in those who do not (or cannot) believe in a Supreme Majesty who has decreed a mission ending in martyrdom, a mission that could only be accomplished by a saint.

Q. Who *exactly* were the followers of La Pucelle?

A. They were the princes of Bourbon and Sarthe with all their peasants. And they numbered La Hire, Dunois, De Rais, Sainte-Sévère, De Xaintrailles and all the other army captains. It was the whole of Brittany led by Richemont, and it was Montmorency with his men who had escaped from the besieged Paris to join the Maid. They were the countless civilian guards and fighters from the towns and villages, the priests with all their parishioners, and the crowds that cheered on Jeanne and her army on their journey to Reims and Paris: men, women, the elderly, children, whole families. They all revered Jeanne, were drunk with longing to see the saint and wanted to touch her. They also supported her materially, as much as they could. All of France, so to speak, mobilised its resources and concentrated on eliminating the enemy.[26]

Q. Who were the enemies of Jeanne d'Arc?

A. First of all the occupying English forces and the Duke of Burgundy, and all their French collaborators. But also the clerks at the universities, the liberal theologians, and the forerunners of the French revolutionaries with their secularised ideas about the sovereignty of the people. Jeanne openly proclaimed the subordination of every temporal office, including that of the king, to the directives of God from whom all power comes. The great saint, in short, defended the Frankish constitution and would have called the French Revolution 'le Grand Mal'.

---

1. Thomas (2000), p.252.
2. Tuchman (1982).
3. I refer to the Council of Basel and to the 'conciliar theories' that circulated in the Church at that time.
4. The cause was the exploitation of workers in the textile industry (Tuchman, 1982, p.61).
5. Virion (1972), p.68.
6. 'Vicar of Christ in the Kingdom of France.' Virion (1972), Chapter II.
7. See Richey (2000), p.17 of 32 of a downloaded file.
8. 'The deep misery of the Kingdom of France.' Fabre (1948, Dutch translation), p.112.
9. Fabre (1948, English translation), p.84.
10. Pernoud (1962), p.95, Richey (2000), p.6 of 32 of a downloaded file.
11. Fabre (1948, English translation), p.85.
12. DeVries (2011), p.70.
13. Pernoud (1962), p.104 (quoting the Bastard of Orléans and Jean d'Aulon).
14. DeVries (2011), p.95.
15. Ibid.
16. DeVries (2011), p.96.
17. Thomas (2000), p.178.
18. Ibid.
19. Roberts (2011), p.28 of 41 of a downloaded file.
20. Ibid.

21. DeVries (2011), p.63.
22. Rehabilitation, 06, p.1 of 9.
23. DeVries (2011), p.65.
24. Liddell Hart, p.50.
25. Virion (1972), p.32.
26. Virion (1972), p.71/72.

11 WAR IN THE MIDDLE AGES

'A just war...served as a basis for exacting feudal aid in the form of men and money. It was of equal importance to have God on your side, because war was considered... as an appeal to the judgment of God.'
- Barbara Tuchman [1]

Thinking of the Middle Ages, we imagine walled cities, fortresses and urban militias.[2] These images stem from the time of the crumbling Carolingian Empire, when the forces of Islam were moving north, invaders came from the east, and the Normans forced cities to construct fortified ramparts. It was a time when Europe was stagnant and threatened from all sides. Only the monasteries kept the flame of civilisation burning. It took until the 12th century for real progress to happen again.

The crusades brought superior construction and siege techniques to Europe. Fortifications and ramparts underwent a change of shape (along the lines of the citadel of Constantinople). For instance, round towers appeared in the outer walls and towns became virtually impenetrable fortresses. Martial art became *the art of besieging*.[3]

Of course, the phenomena 'siege' and 'fortifications' had existed for thousands of years; think of Nineveh and the Great Wall of China. But for the average medieval citizen they were new because the ancient knowledge had been largely lost.[4] In the 8th to the 9th century, Roman walls, roads and viaducts decayed into ruins. The only defence structure was an earthen wall with a moat. Only later fortified bridges appeared, initially made of earth and wood.[5] Only when the Normans besieged Paris did notions of mechanics and ballistics equal the knowledge of the Romans. The ram, the catapult and the moving tower were rediscovered; but the besieged also developed ingenious methods and tools to resist the attackers.[6]

In the 14th century, gunpowder became known in Europe and guns were introduced.[7] Military architecture changed because stone walls could not withstand cannonballs.[8] Fragile tall constructions were therefore replaced by a system of buried reinforcements, surrounded by wide canals.[9] 'Bastions' appeared, fortresses shielded by palisades (of earth and faggots).[10]

Because besieging fortresses could be expensive and difficult [vassals usually were committed for only 40 days per year], taking fortresses *by storm* was the preferred method. For that purpose, the attackers used ladders, mobile towers, climbing nets, various methods to cross moats, and the 'trebuchet', a kind of catapult that used gravity – not tension – to launch projectiles to set fire to the roofs. In the meantime, the besiegers – covered by fire – tunnelled under the walls.[11]

The core of the medieval army in 1300 was knights seated on strong, aggressive stallions and equipped with lances. 'A brave man on a good horse could do more in one hour than ten or perhaps a hundred man on foot' was a prevailing notion.[12] The protection of the cavalier was a compromise between (a) thicker armour (from the 13th century onwards, in response to firearms), (b) arms, and (c) mobility. The same rings true for the tank, the successor to the cavalry. The knight's main weapon was the lance; and for struggle in the turmoil the sword. 'The knights fought in close formations – or in successive lines – to be able to take maximum advantage of the 'shock and awe' and each other's support.'[13] Armies made up of knights rarely numbered more than 1000 men.

The main feature of medieval battle tactics was the breakthrough, especially in the centre. [Armoured knights were much too heavy to quickly attack the enemy on the flanks.] The commanders of the units fought at the front (the supreme commanders did not). If the banner of one of the parties was lost, then the struggle – which usually lasted barely one hour – was over. Without a banner there was no unity or chance to regroup. Therefore Jeanne's standard played a much bigger role than someone from the 21st century might think!

La Pucelle had a large and a small standard. The 'large standard' (80 cm x 3,56 m, possibly longer) was completely white. On one side was an image of Christ seated on a rainbow with two kneeling angels. In his right hand he held a globe while blessing with his left hand a lily that one of the angels presented to him. On the standard was written in gold JESUS MARIA. Furthermore, the white surface at the bottom of the standard was full of depictions of the French lily, symbol of the kings of France. The lance to which the standard was attached was 5.5 m long. The person who had to take the standard into battle had to be strong and agile!

The small, triangular white standard ('pennon') was approximately 80 cm x 1,4 m in size. This standard was attached to a lance of 3 m. Probably both the front and the back depicted an angel presenting Mary with a lily. Accompanying the scene were the words JESUS MARIA. On a white background were golden French lilies.

Finally, Jeanne had a 'banner' to show where the priests were gathering. On this banner was an image of the Crucifixion.[14]

Jeanne d'Arc's battle standard, pennon and banner

The 14th century witnessed the emergence of urban infantry. In the Battle of the Golden Spurs, the Flemish 'infantry' destroyed the French army of knights of Philip the Fair (1302). Such victories were also won elsewhere. [But infantry suffered many defeats as well.] The success of the infantry can be attributed to (a) the impoverishment of the nobility because of the crusades, (b) the success of the cities (accompanied by an increasing self-awareness), and (c) the acquisition of better weapons (the crossbow, longbow, and various other weapons).

Because of these developments, fighters on foot became more and more of a match for the cavalry.[15] Cohesion, solidarity and pride played an important role in all of this because the medieval man did not fight individually but rather in a phalanx; uniforms and flags emphasised this unity.

Prioritising infantry – at the expense of the cavalry – came from the battles in the Holy Land. Richard the Lionheart was at the end of the 12th century far ahead of his time by entrusting a major operation to his infantry. These developments came to the fore in Europe in the French and English armies during the Hundred Years War. However, the English applied these ideas ahead of the French (see Appendix II, the Battle of Verneuil), partly because the knight had kept more of his prestige in France. The French were also slower than the English and Burgundians in grasping the importance of conquering and retaining fortified cities to control the country around them.

That the French persisted with their old, tactically disastrous behaviour until Jeanne arrived is one of the riddles of this time. It has been suggested that tactics always lag behind battle innovations, which may go some way towards explaining matters.[16] [17]

In a battle between foot soldiers and cavalry, the parties first had to organise themselves in the field. Organising the foot soldiers usually took two to three hours. Next, the enemy's cavalry approached to within 200 m. Archers then had 20 seconds to shoot. Two scenarios were conceivable.

In scenario (1), foot soldiers with spears break the charge of the cavalry: horses run into the spears and knights are catapulted off their horses and killed. In scenario (2), the foot soldiers panic, attempt to flee and are trampled underfoot by the horses.[18]

The Battle of Verneuil (1424) was a prototype of a battle between the new English method of fighting and the old French way: 17000 French knights attacked 9000 Englishmen head on while from the first line and the flanks longbowmen launched barrages of arrows towards the attackers.[19] These arrows immediately weakened the charging cavalry. Behind the archers and spears were dismounted knights (who fought on foot, something very new at that time). As soon as the hostile cavalry arrived, the archers withdrew, and the knights braced for the impact.

The use of longbowmen was mainly defensive and this strategy was decisive only when the English were attacked by an opponent who approached them head on over a terrain that complicated his advance, for example uphill.

In the time of Jeanne d'Arc, warfare had changed significantly, notably by the (re) introduction of infantry and the use of cannons and field artillery. In response to the use of the latter[20] the armour became thicker and cities were strengthened with bulwarks and towers. This in turn altered how sieges were conducted.

---

1. Tuchman (1982), p.96.
2. We see these for the first time in northern Italy during the second half of the 12th century. The urban militia included noble knights but primarily

consisted of foot soldiers (which were classified according to neighbourhood, social class or guild). Soon they also appeared in Flanders (especially Ghent had a strong militia) and in the 13th century became influential in the Netherlands.
3. Beaufre (1965), p.60.
4. Newman (1942), p.110.
5. Later examples were made of stone.
6. The weapons of betrayal and starvation were of course always at the disposal of the besiegers; on the other hand, a lengthy siege was very expensive.
7. Newman (1942), p.70/71. See also Fox (2006), p.132.
8. De Vos (2006), p.133.
9. Ibid.
10. Ibid.
11. Later on, with the emergence of effective artillery (15th century), modern fortifications developed; these relied on firepower. High walls disappeared.
12. Tuchman (1982), p.36.
13. De Vos (2006), p.125.
14. https://www.jeanne-darc.info/biography/banner accessed 20 July 2019. A variety of testimonies exist about what the standard and the banner looked like. According to some, a representation of Mary accompanied by a shield, sustained by two angels, could be found on the back of the battle standard, as well as the coat of arms of France. And on the banner – against a blue background – there was (it is sometimes said) a white dove [the Holy Spirit]. The dove had in his beak a pennant with the text 'De par le Roy du Ciel'. All this aside, *only* what Jeanne herself said about the standard during her trial is certain: 'I had a standard with a field littered with lilies; depicted on it was Christ who bore in his hand the globe with an angel on his side; the standard was white in color and of a shiny drapery called boucassin. The names of Jesus and Mary were written on it and the standard had silk fringes.'
15. Knights hated the crossbow because the operator could not see who he killed. They had an even bigger dislike of firearms because with them any bastard could shoot down a 'gentil homme'. Newman (1942), p.33. See also Tuchman (1982), p.110.
16. During the 15th century, there was a trend for experimentation: see the defeat of Charles the Bold against the Swiss when the Swiss (re)*introduced infantry*. Groundbreaking was the invasion of Italy by Charles VIII in 1494, using artillery and Swiss infantrymen. Naples, Venice, Milan and Florence all succumbed; their castles and condottieri could not resist the innovations in the army of Charles VIII.
17. DeVries, p.147.
18. A battle between foot soldiers usually lasted two to three hours and

generally involved a struggle between several thousand combatants resulting in hundreds of deaths. Foot soldiers tended to act defensively and seldom pursued the enemy.
19. The difference between a crossbow and a longbow is that the crossbow is more powerful, but that the (cheaper) longbow allows the soldier to fire 10-13 arrows per minute. It remains a mystery why the French did not develop adequate protection against these barrages (Thomas, 2000, p.31).
20. Cannons and artillery strengthened offensive capabilities.

12 THE FRENCH ARMY

'A soldier, at any rate of time of peace, is 'only a civilian armed in a particular manner."
- English maxim[1]

The feudal army was a product of medieval society. War was a moral and religious concept, 'an ordeal in which the participants had to meet each other under equal and fair conditions'.[2] The traditional rules and moral codes of chivalry were still applicable.[3] Thus, one did not attack someone's land when he was imprisoned,[4] no acts of war were committed on holy days,[5] and the war had to be 'justified' (or at least have the appearance of being so). Jeanne d'Arc acted entirely in this spirit given her respect for the opponent and the jus belli. For example, the Maid had mass said for prisoners and warned the English three times before she attacked. La Pucelle was perfectly medieval in this respect.

The feudal system regulated the legal and economic side of the relationship between suzerain and vassal. Only services/goods were exchanged – no money. The services were personal and performed on demand. [The feudal system did not revolve around abstractions and legal fabrications (as in a democracy) but addressed concrete and lived relationships between men.]

In the Middle Ages armies were only assembled in response to specific issues, given that a vassal was only obliged to serve for a certain number of days of the year (usually 40). This temporary character stood in the way of discipline but also prevented the boundlessness of the later Napoleonic Wars.[6]

In the time of Jeanne d'Arc, i.e. the late Middle Ages, the French 'army' was not under a clear, central, royal command. The constable, for example, was a mighty man who, with his own army, did what he wanted, independently of the royal will. Otherwise, what is here referred to as an 'army' was rather an unruly collection of individual units. From the collapse of the feudal system (i.e. from the 12th century onwards), these units did not have a real master except for the relevant 'captain' – hired by the king – who recruited his own soldiers (their contract did not call for heroic deeds).

Due to the rapid spread of money – and later capitalism – the original institution of feudal service was gradually replaced by pecuniary motives. As a result, permanent and professional armies sprung up. This development could be witnessed particularly in the Italian city-states.[7] Many knights now saw warfare as a possibility to earn money and offered themselves – with their men – to wealthy cities and traders, something that would have been unthinkable during the heyday of the Middle Ages.[8]

The power balance between the rulers and the relatively un-bloody wars, all that disappeared. Wars became shorter, more bitter and bloodier due to the increased firepower of the artillery (which made it easier to kill).[9] More infantry also meant fewer fighters drawn from the higher echelons of society, which lowered the social status of the army. The ideal of the chivalrous knight was dead.

---

1. Cited in Wheeler-Bennett (1954), p.3/4.
2. Earle (1960), p.14.
3. Tuchman (1982), p.84 et sequens
4. The English did just this in the case of Duke Charles of Orléans.
5. The English did just this during the siege of Orléans; they opened fire on 17 October.
6. Including both the World Wars.
7. It was in these cities that the phenomenon of 'condottieri' (mercenaries) first emerged.
8. De Vos (2006), p.39.
9. See Earle (1960).

13 WOMEN IN THE ARMY

'To go wrong on the fundamental problem of 'man and woman', to deny the most abysmal antagonism between them and the necessity of an eternally hostile tension, to dream perhaps of equal rights, equal education, equal claims and obligations - that is a typical sign of shallowness.'
- Friedrich Nietzsche

Women were absent from the medieval armies. They were considered unsuitable to be 'killers'. Moreover, the ideal of the knight who fought for his lady still existed in the late Middle Ages. Only in desperate situations (when communities were threatened[1]) and/or if men were missing or failing, women played a role. This is generally true of warfare. Only occasionally have situations emerged where women lead military operations; and even more sporadic are women who kill in battle.

Often, female warriors were the wives of kings, or in similar positions of power; as in the case of Deborah and Judith in the

Old Testament, and Boudicca in the struggle of the English Celts against the Romans. However, whether these women – the martially artful Judith excepted – really fought and killed in the frontline is questionable. Most women who were in uniform on the battlefield or who boarded naval ships were women who followed their loved ones.[2] Others were women who, with their men, defended their home and hearth (and sometimes a whole city) against outside aggression.

[All this does not contradict the fact that in history there have been aggressive women, some with great power. I am thinking of Christina of Sweden, Catherine the Great, Maria-Theresia, Golda Meir and Margaret Thatcher. However, they all left actual war to the professionals.[3] Only a certain Artemisia (who lived between 300 BCE and 100 CE, Mabille van Bellem (11th century), 'Belle Boyd' (an American patriot in the civil war)[4], and a few more are *certified* warriors, i.e. individuals who have killed other individuals in a direct confrontation.[5]]

Jeanne d'Arc reminds us of the Dutch Jenny Merkus (the 'Jeanne d'Arc of the Balkans') and the Russian Nasezha Durova. The first was a fanatic, not without courage, but by no means a commander and not a strategic thinker at all. The latter – unlike La Pucelle – was simply a terrible commander. Women were and are – with a few exceptions – not present at the level of 'Grand Strategy'.[6]

If we compare Jeanne d'Arc to men, then the Maid has more in common with Rommel (as far as leadership is concerned) and Otto Skorzeny, the charismatic commander of the special forces in Hitler's empire who, at one point, was the most dangerous man in Europe.[7]

About Nasezha Durova:

This female warrior, of rural descent and born in 1790, walked away from her husband, disguised as a man; she wanted from the outset to become a warrior and 'son' of her father (whom she loved). She craved the independent existence of a soldier and enlisted in the tsar's army. Durova was present at the battle of Friedland (1807) and at the battle of Borodino (1812). When she was caught, she was brought to St. Petersburg and interviewed by a curious Tsar Alexander I. On this occasion she asked him to be permitted to stay in the army because there was nothing in the world she wanted more than to be a 'soldier, in uniform and armed'. Durova was sent back to her regiment and used by the authorities for propaganda purposes. It is said that she hated her own sex, that she operated completely without fear, but that she was timid and frightened of lonely places, shadows and unexpected noises. Moreover, she never killed anyone – just like Jeanne.

There have always been women soldiers (usually dressed as men), especially in the Americas of the 19th century. Often these female soldiers served to apparent satisfaction. This was the case with Loreta Velázquez, a patriot for the Confederates in the American Civil War, who followed her husband into the army. There are more of such cases,[8] but they are anecdotal and insignificant. Even in the Red Army there was among all those millions of soldiers only one woman who drove a tank.[9]

In revolutions and rebellions women play a larger role than in regular military operations; throughout history, women have been involved in revolutions to the tune of around 12.5%.[10] Even among them one finds remarkably few commanders. Thus, in the Israeli partisans' organisation Palmach, no woman commanded a unit that was larger than a patrol.[11]

According to Creveld (2001) there are two reasons that explain the higher percentage of women in revolutions and rebellions. Firstly, women generate less suspicion and are treated less mercilessly than men. Secondly, in revolutions and rebellions the circumstances are so different from ordinary life that men can fight alongside a few women without losing their self-esteem; however, once the freedom fighters come out into the open, the women disappear.

Most of the great stories about female warriors – think of Mulan and the Amazons – belong to mythology, except for the Dahomey Amazons. But even in this case it is difficult to separate fact from fiction. Creveld (2001) states about the following about the Dahomey Amazons: 'To become a warrior, they had, as they said themselves, to surrender their womanhood, turn into men, and despise women. To the extent that this is based on facts, their fate was neither laughable nor enviable but simply tragic.'[12] During a royal parade, one of the Dahomey warriors once gave a speech that began with the following words: 'As the blacksmith bends an iron rod with fire, so we have changed our way of being. We are men, not women.'

'War,' writes Martin van Creveld elsewhere, 'is not a matter for women.' Sure, I say, and Jeanne d'Arc is the exception that confirms this rule.

In today's world, focused on gender equality, the role of women in the army (and in war) *seemingly* has become more important. For instance, in the 1980s, in the name of *affirmative action*, an obsessive policy of 'positive discrimination' was deployed in the US. Through intelligent labelling, the preferential treatment of women was linked to race. Sexism and racism were asserted to come from the same root.[13] In reality, affirmative action was an absurd administrative measure that generated absurdity.[14] The best were no longer chosen: competence was sacrificed to political correctness and the quality of the chosen candidates decreased. Soldiers and firefighters complained[15] that the physical requirements for women were lower so that when push came to shove, the men had to do the physical work. Admission systems and promotion schemes became lotteries in which government officials ignored objective data such as physical strength, diplomas, years served and aversion to risk in favour of racial or gender related criteria.

[In this context I remember a wonderful comment I saw on the internet from a British paratrooper: 'If women want to stand in a Hercules aircraft being airsick carrying 160 lb. of equipment, jump and land on rough ground at night, then speed-march 50 miles in 24 hours before even meeting the enemy, good luck to them.']

In October 1994 an American female pilot crashed on landing on an aircraft carrier. While the US navy officially told the world that the accident was due to a mechanical defect, it was generally known that it was due to pilot error. The female pilot in question could pursue her training despite seven crashes in simulated combat situations (a male pilot would have been disqualified after a few crashes). Why? Because an admiral had announced under political pressure that he wanted to have more women in combat roles.

Despite affirmative action, according to Creveld (2001), in no country the absolute dominance of men in the army has been even remotely affected.[16] Solid evidence for this fact is that almost all casualties are men.[17]

---

1. In August 2014 this applied to societies (e.g. the Kurds) that were threatened by ISIS.

2. Forty (1997), p.56. Garibaldi, for example, had a woman like that.
3. See Creveld (2001). The same may apply to Boudicca.
4. See Forty (1997), p.49/55.
5. For more about female warriors see Forty (1997).
6. In religious terms, Jeanne resembles Judith from the old Testament. See also Virion (1972), p.9.
7. Skorzeny was the man who, on 12 September 1943, was responsible for the liberation of Mussolini (on the mountain Gran Sasso) from the hands of the Badoglio government.
8. See *Women War Heroines* by George and Anne Forty (1997).
9. See Creveld (2001), p.102/104 and p.143.
10. Creveld (2001), p.117.
11. Creveld (2001), p.120.
12. Creveld (2001), p.116.
13. This linking together of the two is completely unjustified. Between man and woman, a difference exists that does not exist between a white and a black man. The difference in the latter case is just a hereditary DNA variation. But the difference between man and woman is irrefutably fundamental: a whole chromosome is different with all the consequences that entails.
14. Hamburg (1995).
15. Thereby jeopardising their careers!
16. Creveld (2001), p.301.
17. Ibid.

14 JEANNE D'ARC'S GRAND STRATEGY

'The terrible Ifs accumulate.'
- Winston Churchill

'Grand Strategy' is nothing but 'value focused' thinking.[1] This form of cognitive activity explicitly starts with an ultimate value. The main idea is to analyse its rational implications so that goals and objectives are brought into a compatible, consistent and hierarchical order,[2] all the while discounting political, diplomatic, economic, military, moral and ethical contexts, and taking into account the magnitude of the factor 'human resources'. A strategy devised on the basis of this type of thinking, when applied in life-threatening conflict situations, aims to break the enemy's will as the highest *concrete* objective. Other goals can only be achieved when we can impose our will on the enemy.[3]

For instance, Hitler's strategic main objective was the conquest and destruction of Leningrad, the cradle of Bolshevism;[4] secondarily he wanted to obtain the raw materials of Ukraine and the oilfields of the Caucasus. But to reach those goals, he first had to impose his will, i.e. destroy the Red Army.[5]

The definition of Grand Strategy given here looks simple but is most complicated, especially when one considers the *quantitative* aspects of this form of thinking. [Think of 'opportunities' expressed in 'uncertainties'.] In order to discount a simple view of 'Grand Strategy', I point out that the military leadership of Japan during World War II was not able to discount 'the full spectrum of political, economic, and international issues', even though the Japanese army and navy had excellent – albeit too small – intelligence units. In the first phase of the war, at the tactical level (i.e. in the short term), the Japanese made very good use of them (think of Pearl Harbor).[6] But at the higher level of Grand Strategy, the Japanese leadership fell short, partly because they confused *expectation* with *logical analysis*. They therefore believed that the Germans would win the Battle of Britain and in the 'rapprochement' of Germany and Russia (just prior to the German invasion of Russia).[7]

Without further commentary I let my warning against underestimating Grand Strategy be accompanied by a remark made by Alan Brooke in a letter to Montgomery (both Field Marshals), a remark to the detriment of General Eisenhower: 'I have (always) shared your opinion,' writes Brooke in this letter, 'that Ike was not a commander, that he did not have a strategic vision, that he was unable to design a plan or to lead the operations if they had begun.'[8]

These introductory remarks contribute to an accurate assessment of the 'Grand Strategy' and respect for the capacities of Jeanne d'Arc in this field![9]

The first task in designing a Grand Strategy is to discover the Achilles heel of the enemy.[10] Then the strategist must centre all the resources of a nation on this weakness.[11] The military is in principle only one of the means. In addition, the strategists have at their disposal propaganda, sanctions, blockages, and diplomacy. The military victory in this 'value focused' thinking is therefore not an inevitable goal in itself. However, all means, including military, find their common goal in breaking the enemy's will, an objective that is located in 'the mind of the enemy command'.[12]

For Jeanne d'Arc, the Achilles heel of the English was the regicide that brought Henry IV to the throne. After a regicide, no king could legally claim the French crown in Catholic Europe of that time. God does not allow the central institution of 'God's city' (= the world)' to be defiled by an unlawful, 'would be', king. That Charles VII – unlike his English opponent – was the legitimate heir to the crown could be affirmed by his coronation and anointing, an event that at the same time could break the will of the English at the deepest level. The aforementioned sacred ceremony not only conferred the right to rule sanctioned by divine authority, but also marked the holder of that power with the semblance and character of Christ himself.[13] *Breaking the English will by means of 'le Sacre du Dauphin' was* **the focus** *in Jeanne's operational phase of her Grand Strategy.*[14]

Of course, the term Grand Strategy did not exist in the time of Jeanne d'Arc, if only because the economic and political dimensions of it had not yet fully developed.[15] Even Napoleon spoke merely of a 'grand tactique'. It was only in the interbellum period that things changed fundamentally. Then the American

Industrial College of the Armed Forces began to instil more knowledge of the economic aspects (of war) into officers.[16]

In addition, there was no 'state' that could develop, finance, integrate and focus economic and political factors and tools of diplomacy on the enemy, even if there have certainly been warlords who were not blind to the power of the economy (e.g. Hannibal, Scipio, Caesar, Cromwell and Napoleon).[17] So, when we talk about a Grand Strategy of La Pucelle, then we talk about such a strategy in embryonic form. Even so, Jeanne heralded something different because medieval warfare did not aim for a strategic victory. In those days, it was rather 'a grasp of power...by damaging as much as possible [whereby] the opponent's fall was accomplished.'[18]

In addition to the 'focus' of breaking the enemy's will, a Grand Strategy – as mentioned – involves a further, **ultimate goal**. This final, ultimate goal corresponds to the 'strategic decision context', i.e. the collection of all conceivable alternatives available to the decision maker. [The separate decisions over time are the 'means through which strategic objectives are pursued.] This ultimate strategic goal is *not* an 'objective' – it is too vague – but a 'value statement'. For the *immediate* reality – a more limited time space – the strategic decision context is too broad. To cope with this immediate reality the strategic decision frame is reduced to a smaller and more concrete decision space. And in this concrete, *operational*, fact-dominated 'decision space' breaking the will of the enemy is the 'focus'.

Q. What was the ultimate goal of Jeanne d'Arc?

A. Breaking the English will by crowning le Dauphin was

certainly a very fundamental objective, an achievement that would have an impact long after Jeanne's death. An even more fundamental goal was the merger of 'national politics' and 'the belief in a unique French reality', a fusion that our great saint, in imitation of Clovis, Pepin and Charlemagne, would proclaim and defend.[19] However, the ultimate goal for Jeanne was carrying out the will of God, the proclamations of 'La Royauté de Notre Seigneur Jésus-Christ'. She *first* did this in front of Braudicourt ('Le royaume n'appartient pas au Dauphin, il appartient à mon Seigneur'[20]), *then* bluntly to the king in Chinon ('serez lieutenant du roi des cieux qui est roi de France'[21]), and *finally* in Poitiers, Blois, Orléans and Reims with various statements along the same lines.[22] Jeanne said this *without ever having a theocracy in mind*. Would the opposite have been true, then it would have been pointless to crown the king according to sacred tradition. No, for Jeanne it was merely a question of a universal legislative, executive and juridical power that belongs only to the 'Roi du Ciel' and which He – without reducing the role of other nations – exercises on a particular people in a very special way.[23] It is exactly this mystical idea that still lives on in the French people, i.e. the idea that the French nation occupies a special place in the world, that 'La France' is the heart of Europe, and that *Gallica Christiane* originates in the baptism[24] of Clovis, king of the Franks, a ground-breaking event in the history of Europe.[25]

With modern knowledge – but without taking her out of her context – one can find in the strategy of the Maid the following elements that makes it essentially a Grand Strategy:

- Jeanne fought a 'just war'. She fought for the existence and integrity of her country and spoke about 'la bonne querelle du royaume de France'.[26] Jacques Gélu, archbishop of Embrun and a contemporary of Jeanne, said: 'The deeds of Jeanne have a useful and righteous purpose, namely: the pacification of the kingdom of France.'[27]
- The French national heroine effectively scuppered the plans of Henry V, imperialist *avant la lettre*. She did this through superior, multi-dimensional thinking.
- To accomplish the fundamental objective of breaking the will of the enemy, Jeanne used a non-military means (the coronation of the king). Jeanne d'Arc thus made use of the psyche and the spirit over a longer period of time, which is characteristic of strategy.
- The French saint brought a religious element to politics, a 'grand strategic' moment par excellence. By referring to eternal values, she deliberately ignored the emerging revolutionary spirit; this purged the notion of sovereignty of secular blemishes[28] and restored the bond between faith and political morality. [That the centuries that came afterwards did not see the point of religion and replaced God with economics is quite another matter.] With the restoration of political and theological unity, Jeanne also defended the 'Latinité' (represented by the party of Charles VII) against the proto-protestant, Anglo-Saxon spirit that already permeated the University of Paris and would result in the schismatic Henry VIII.[29]
- Jeanne's already looked to the future, to the time after the liberation of France when she saw herself fighting

the heretical Hussites. This she did at the age of 17, without any training, straight from the farm!

There are five other striking facets to Jeanne's strategy, namely: (A) restoring royal authority by fighting the chaos, (B) not waging war on two fronts, (C) the strategic significance of Compiègne, (D) the importance of moral factors, and (E) the benefits of the offensive.

A: *Restoring royal authority by fighting the chaos*

Jeanne realised that she needed to get to the bottom of the disastrous situation in France. The chaos, looting and raping etc. could be traced back to a lack of royal authority. Her 'focus' (or overall fundamental objective) is therefore not breaking the Siege of Orléans (which is only an 'intermediate objective'), but the crowning and anointing of the king in Reims so that the morale ('the will') of the English will be broken while that of the French will be boosted.[30]

A complete structuring of objectives can be achieved by constructing a system of 'hierarchies' and 'networks'. For instance, there are 'fundamental objectives hierarchies' and 'networks of intermediate objectives' [= the modelled whole of objectives that relate the alternatives (causally) to their consequences]. The aforementioned hierarchies and networks can be fused together. In that form, the form of a 'decision space', they serve as the basis of decision models (among which one finds 'decision trees' and 'influence diagrams'). 'Overall fundamental objectives' are objectives that are common to both the hierarchy and the network. This is where the *interface* between concept and implementation, between macro and micro level, is located. It is the level of the *operational strategy*. At this level of intertwining between 'thought and virtue' on the one hand, and 'reason, spirit and genius' on the other, complexity is exceedingly large, and developments are no longer predictable.

The endpoint of the top-down structuring of a fundamental objectives hierarchy is reached at the level at which reasonable 'attributes' are found. [An attribute is the benchmark for determining the degree to which an objective has been reached.] However, what is reasonable? The answer is 'what reason prescribes', i.e. what is dictated by a rationally directed consciousness (this consciousness is always a mix of thought and emotion, but the proportions vary).

To be clear: designating her 'focus' (= 'overall' fundamental objective) was a **political and psychological** decision by Jeanne. Her 'operational' strategy was entirely focused on breaking the will of the English through the crowning and anointing of Charles VII. That was her mission. The idea that the Maid was only a brave soldier is thereby refuted. Stephen Richey (2000) also sees things in this way: Jeanne's decision was a 'national policy' decision, a decision that was taken by a 'peasant girl' who imposed her will on the indecisive Dauphin.[31]

Montgomery wrote: 'Unless there is a sharply defined political goal in military plans, war only results in a useless slaughter.'[32] Regine Pernoud (1962) also recognises the strategic significance of the king's crowning and anointing. She acknowledges that La Pucelle took all her 'operationally strategic' decisions guided by 'le Sacre du Dauphin'. 'Once the king is crowned in a sacred way,' the Maid used to say, 'then the king shall be king for all.'[33]

The people around the king hated Jeanne's ideas. After all, her strategy was diametrically opposed to theirs and moreover risky [because the French army had to travel across Anglo-Burgundian territory, where it could encounter English garrisons and groups of wandering brigands]. Hence many of the king's advisors would rather have attacked Normandy. However, nobody could make La Pucelle change her mind: 'We must go to Reims. In Reims, the noble Dauphin must be crowned and be anointed; after the anointing, the power of the enemy will collapse, and he will not be able to hurt the king and the kingdom.'[34] Of course, to ensure that the Dauphin could be crowned, any English resistance on the way to Reims had to be extinguished. Hence the need for the clearing of the Loire and its banks. Orléans had to be relieved immediately, because with the fall of that city the kingdom of Charles VII (who already considered fleeing to Le Dauphiné, Spain or Scotland) would be directly threatened.[35]

The choice between Normandy or Reims, according to Heinz Thomas (2000), came down to the difference between the armoured chest of the English (Normandy) and the exposed belly of the Anglo-Burgundian alliance (Reims).[36] The latter situation was very well known to Jeanne.[37] In retrospect, this is easy to see for everyone. But the question is why so many others did not see the sense of what Jeanne was saying or did not want to accept it. Was it purely a case of devious advisors trying to stop La Pucelle to remain in power? Because in the end, the coronation in Reims was unmistakably 'a masterful move on the political chessboard'.[38]

The ceremony was not indispensable; after all, your royal blood makes you king. But the mystery of the coronation made the whole trip to Reims powerful. And when it came to breaking the will there was indeed no better strategic objective than 'le Sacre du Dauphin'.

Jeanne's 'focus' was breaking the will of the English[39] through the coronation ceremony. This was God's will, and the Maid did nothing but obey heaven. Of course, she also had to act in real time. Because of her 'value focused' thinking, all her interim objectives were operationally dominated by the 'overall fundamental objective' (= 'focus') of breaking the English will by crowning and anointing the king.

B: *Not waging war on two fronts*

Jeanne knew that she had to avoid fighting on two fronts. That is why she tried to reconcile Charles VII and Philip the Good. She sent at least two letters to the Burgundian monarch in which she asked him to make peace with Charles VII. But the Duke of Burgundy refused. [Hitler also knew that one should not fight on two fronts, but he could not substantiate his knowledge. However, American strategists plan for the US to be able to fight and win in two war-theatres.]

C: *The strategic significance of Compiègne*

Given the plans of the Duke of Burgundy, it was necessary to conquer Paris. [Philip was purely after territorial expansion – all his treaties with Charles VII were phony.][40] In addition, our visionary heroine also wanted to secure the line Creil-Soissons in order to pre-empt an attack by Bedford and Philip of Burgundy on the land of Orléans.[41]

Jeanne was the only one with access to the king who saw the strategic importance of Compiègne.[42] But the words of La Pucelle fell on deaf ears. It was the loyalty of the inhabitants of Compiègne that preserved this city for Charles VII, not the chatter of Regnault de Chartres who was willing to give the city to Philip the Good. Had the latter happened, then the history of France and the whole of Europe certainly would have been different.[43] The English would have reconquered the areas they had lost and France, without its national dynasty and Roman faith, would have suffered Protestantism a century later. France would have become heretical in the eyes of Rome.[44]

This projection is supported by the fact that in 1566 (!) the Protestants of Rouen regarded themselves as subjects of the English kings, as if nothing had happened since the liberation of Orléans. They were willing to bring Dieppe, Rouen and Le Havre under the authority of Calais which the English still had at that time. If it had been up to the Huguenots, the Catholic monarchy of France would have been ruthlessly replaced by a republic à la Genève under Calvin.[45] *The work of Jeanne d'Arc, including her death, can therefore be seen as a bolstering the universal Church of Rome.*

D: *Moral factors are crucial*

In agreement with Clausewitz, the founder of modern military thinking, Jeanne saw the supreme importance of moral factors. An army without discipline and 'a culture of war' degenerates into a deadly, pillaging gang. Especially Jeanne's policy against camp followers should be seen in this light.

In *The Culture of War*, Creveld (2008) mentions four examples of such 'hordes:' (1) the Roman latrones (who were something in-between criminals and enemies of the state[46]), (2) the rebellions of escaped slaves (including those of Spartacus, 73-70 BCE), (3) the Jacquerie (a peasant uprising in France in May 1358 which was brutally crushed[47]) and (4) the many dozens of militias in the more recent conflict in Bosnia-Herzegovina.

Simply believing in a 'good cause' is insufficient. It is a matter of strong fighting spirit and a strong *esprit de corps*. Napoleon expressed it thus: 'The morale is to the physical as three to one.'[48] Moreover, Clausewitz wrote: 'No matter how much one may be inclined to take the most sophisticated view of war, it would be a serious mistake to underrate professional pride ('esprit de corps') as something that may and must be present in an army to greater or lesser degree.'[49] It is indeed this 'esprit de corps' that keeps the cohesion of a group when the group is under fire or hears rumours.[50] The French general Beaufre (1965) endorsed this wisdom with the following statement: 'An army is an organized mob and the cement which binds it together is discipline and mutual confidence.'[51] Clausewitz also wrote: ...moral elements are among the most important in war. They constitute the spirit that permeates war as a whole, and at an early stage they establish a close affinity with the will [of the commander] that moves and leads the whole mass of force...'[52]

One of the first moral considerations is *discipline*. This was crucial for Jeanne. According to d'Alençon, she was 'very angry when she heard soldiers swearing'. She often yelled at them, including her 'gentil Duc'. When d'Alençon saw her, he bridled his swearing immediately.[53] But Jeanne's demands did not stop there. She made her men confess prior to battle, drove prostitutes from the camp and forbade the usual plundering.[54] Concerning the latter, here is the testimony of Simon Baucroix: 'In war time, she would not permit any of those in her company to steal anything; nor would she ever eat of food which she knew to be stolen.' Reginald Thierry, the king's court physician, backs this up: 'When the town of Saint-Pierre-le-Moustier was taken, by assault...the soldiers wanted to pillage the church...but Jeanne prohibited and forbade them with great energy...'[55]

There is more to be said about La Pucelle's thinking on this subject. Our heroine must – for instance – have known that the use of field artillery as an instrument to strike terror into the enemy weakened the morale of the defenders.[56] [The hail of arrows from the English archers had the same purpose.] This psychological effect was harnessed by Jeanne at Orléans and in the early stages before the walls of Paris (which also gave her cover to explore the walls in search of the weakest spot). At Troyes, even the threat of using artillery had an effect. However, undermining morale is not always the outcome of such measures. The bombing of English and German cities during the Second World War strengthened the morale of the victims. The same goes for Saddam Hussein's SCUD missiles targeting Israel. On the other hand, in *Operation Desert Storm* (1991) the Iraqi army was disoriented and demoralised by a 39-day bombardment. Finally, the impression of an unstoppable *Loire offensive* had in itself a deeply demoralising effect on the English.

E: *Benefits of the offensive*

Overall, La Pucelle's strategy was offensive. After all, Jeanne had the explicit intention to invade occupied territory with an army to eliminate the opponent and break his will.[57] Her strategic plan was to carry out a forward movement with power and speed, and this was accompanied by matching tactics.[58] Admittedly, Jeanne does not order a *tactical* attack the day after the conquest of Les Tourelles when the English and French faced each other in the field. This non-action resulted rather from her prudence and her awareness of a possible ruse from the English as well as her respect for the Lord's Day. Characteristic of La Pucelle's tactical thinking, then, is not her occasional passiveness but her continuous desire for immediate, frontal attack.

There are additional benefits of a direct attack that carry weight at the *strategic* level:[59]

- The one who attacks controls the will and the thoughts

of the opponent (who experiences more hesitation and uncertainty than the attacker).
- The moral force is increased because uncertainty has a depressing effect. The offensive troops usually have more confidence in their leader than the defensive troops. Therefore, the defenders should take the initiative back as soon as possible, i.e. fight back.
- Fighting on enemy territory (and the conquest of it) brings profit.[60]

Here are some famous quotes about offensive action:

- 'The ultimate intention must be an offensive one' (Sir William Slim, general).
- 'A revolutionary war...regards offensive activities as the most essential' (General Vo Nguen Giap).
- 'We were never on the defensive, except by accident and in error' (Lawrence of Arabia).
- 'We can conquer only by attacking' (General Patton).
- 'The attack is not only the most effective and but (also) the easiest form of warfare and the moral difference between advance and retreat is simply incalculable. Even when inferior in numbers, it pays to be as aggressive as possible' (General Wavell).[61]

In almost all military situations, La Pucelle operated offensively. In almost every battle, Jeanne personally led the attack. Of this offensive attitude she testified in her response to the king when they were speaking of the conduct of Catherine La Rochelle, a rival visionary who claimed – through appearances of a 'woman in white' – to get instructions from heaven, in this case to generate money to pay Jeanne's soldiers. Catharine was less combative and rather inclined to the diplomatic game. For La Pucelle this did not make sense. 'You will find no peace,' she said to the king: 'save at the lance's point.'[62] In short, just like Rommel during the Second World War, Jeanne was able to permeate all the ranks of her army with her offensive spirit.[63]

Distinguish within the strategic-offensive intention the *tactical* issue of the 'frontal attack' (Jeanne) versus the 'indirect approach'. In the latter an actor attacks his enemy only when he is shocked, surprised and out of balance, for example because he is approached from an unexpected direction.[64] This 'indirect approach' is in particular a good choice for the party that knows he is not strong enough to defeat the enemy on a site chosen by the latter.

At the heart of the indirect approach lies the idea that the imbalance between the opponents before the fight can be balanced by manoeuvres that limit all-out fighting. Actually, the indirect approach relies on the element of surprise.

The landing of the Allies in North Africa in 1942, according to Beaufre (1965), is a good example of an indirect approach.[65] *The attack by Rommel on Tobroek is also an example of this.*

Jeanne without a doubt was an advocate of direct confrontation.[66] *But not always*! [For that reason alone, is it not easy to classify her as the type of strategist that has only one principle, namely 'attack'.[67]] When she came face to face with the English army at Orléans, she forbade the French to attack. The main force of the royal army was not even involved in the Battle of Patay. In addition, Jeanne's operational strategy – which centred on the coronation– was rather *psychological* (to achieve a 'dislocation' in the mind of the opponent). Now, in a strategic model, there are levels: starting from the Grand

Strategic goal, the closer one comes to the reality of the actual battlefield, the more one approaches the 'interface' between strategy (concept) and tactics (implementation) – the level of 'operational strategy'. With these different levels, the composition of the elements of the strategy becomes different. Overall, it is not easy to characterise Jeanne's actions and thinking because in Jeanne La Pucelle strategy and tactics were united.

Jeanne's direct confrontations demanded many lives [characteristic of frontal attacks!]. But according to military historian DeVries (2011), they were more effective than any other method in halting the English momentum.[68] Sure, it's an ironclad strategy, but it involves a calculated risk and when successful it wipes out all other factors and assures the collapse of all pockets of resistance. General Patton thought similarly: 'Violent attacks, although costly at the time, save lives in the end.'[69] Creveld says the same in other words: 'In a struggle most hits are probably handed out too late rather than too early. By the time of intervention, one is already so accustomed to killing that [in terms of effectiveness] the hits add little more. Conversely, the longer you wait, the more barbarian the methods you apply.'[70]

Reflecting on Jeanne's strategic thinking, the following points are central:

- The great heroine of France embodied the central authority/controlling will/driving force; she made – until Reims – the will of Charles VII subordinate to hers.
- She personified the unity, ingenuity and daring of the highest army command.

- She understood the enemy psychologically (especially Philip the Good).
- She knew that the relationship between resources and purpose should be proportional; consider how she did not besiege La Charité-sur-Loire due to insufficient resources.[71]
- She did not experience any uncertainty (listening obediently to her voices). However, the other army commanders were dealing with the 'fog of war' and with the estimation of probabilities, the latter without the mathematical and statistical apparatus, including game theory, that is available to today's generals. Of course, the commanders of the French army wanted to limit their uncertainties, for 'whoever dallies with danger will perish in it'.[72] But how? By simply trusting La Pucelle, which they did.

No one can explain Jeanne's strategic knowledge.[73] No one can explain how the holy girl was able to make the right choices in unknown terrain (like the banks of the Loire between Blois and Orléans). No one can explain Jeanne's insight into the effects of the coronation of Le Dauphin. But all that knowledge and intuition were undeniable there. That she impressed her fellow commanders is a fact. After Orléans she had an undeniable influence over military decisions. After Patay the army commanders fully acknowledged her superiority in the field of warfare. D'Alençon found her an exquisite strategist and praised the way she positioned the artillery.

Her advice to Braudicourt to not give battle before the end of Lent reveals an absolutely miraculous strategic knowledge because (1) the French would undoubtedly have fallen into the trap of the English troop arrangement, and (2) the French would have time to develop a new attitude towards war. Moreover, Jeanne saw that the shares of infantry and artillery had to increase drastically before the army of the Dauphin could face future battles with confidence.

All existing sources confirm that the saint of Orléans had an innate strategic and tactical knowledge that enabled her to operate as a chess player on the battlefield. 'Jeanne,' agrees the typically critical Taylor (2010), 'was a warrior, a soldier and a general.'[74]

Note that after Melun, where in April 1430 Jeanne's saints tell her that she will be captured ('Il faut que tu sois prise'), the Maid makes no more decisions.

In conclusion:

The 'overall' fundamental objective of Jeanne's Grand Strategy can be said to have been the mystic nature of the coronation of Charles VII. This strategy is considered a daring feat of military and political thinking. Jeanne single-handedly achieved a unique moral, psychological and emotional mobilisation of the French nation. She awakened the national identity of the people and turned it into unity. Meanwhile, she conquered cities and won back lost terrain. She was truly a freedom warrior of the highest rank. But the ultimate goal of her mission – according to her own statements – was the proclamation of 'La Royauté de notre seigneur Jésus-Christ'.

---

1. A form of creative thinking in which problems are seen as possibilities to create 'opportunities'. The pay-off of the value-focused approach, which is systematised by directives, consists in obtaining – ultimately – more attractive consequences.
2. Cf. Baylis et al. (1975), p.18.
3. Liddell Hart (1944), p.151.

4. Rees (2013), p.253.
5. See Rooyen (2013), p.401. See also Manstein, quoted in Connelly (2002), p.143 and Rees (2013), p. 254. Only much later did Hitler accept the army heading towards Moscow.
6. Kotani (2009).
7. Kotani (2009), p.160.
8. Gardner (1964), p.19.
9. One needs to distinguish at the strategic level between 'direct' and 'indirect'. The difference between these can be explained as follows: when a party believes that there are too few resources to opt for a direct (military) confrontation, it does well to choose an indirect strategy. Such a strategy seeks to achieve a result other than through – purely – military victory. [In such a strategy, psychology always plays a major role, for example through the morale of the opponent, or through manipulations when international reactions affect the outcome.] Maritime powers, in particular, use the indirect strategy to bring the opponent down (logistically) through maritime power (and thus keep their land forces in reserve). But also Mao Tse-Tung successfully applied indirect methods to exhaust the enemy.

    The indirect strategy maintains maximum freedom of action. Important thereby is that in such a strategy the focus of the fight is no longer on actual battles. Thus, Jeanne's intended coronation mysticism was indeed a form of indirect strategy, but one that was accompanied by a direct approach at the tactical level. The indirect strategy is especially emphasised by Liddell Hart (1944). André Beaufre, commander of the French Army in Suez in 1957, sees in Liddell Hart's indirect strategy and Clausewitz's thoughts on direct military victory representatives of two doctrines that do not have universal validity. 'Each of these doctrines,' writes Beaufre (1965), 'will be the best in certain circumstances and the worst imaginable in other circumstances.' Only the current situation on the ground will determine which doctrine should be followed. It is not ruled out that various doctrines can follow each other. It is certain, according to Beaufre, that strategy is no longer a matter of purely history and objective deduction, but also of making use of hypotheses, reflection, guided creativity, and truly original thoughts. Nowadays it is simply necessary to be well-informed, creative and proactive.
10. Liddell Hart (1944), p.152.
11. Ibid.
12. Liddell Hart (1944), p.48.
13. Virion (1972), p.163.
14. 'The inauguration (and anointing) of the Dauphin.'
15. Not to mention psychology and sociology.
16. Creveld (2007), p.172/73. Something similar also happened in Germany around the same time.

17. Liddell Hart (1944), p.56.
18. Tuchman (1982), p.104.
19. Virion (1972), p.63.
20. 'The kingdom does not belong to le Dauphin, it belongs to my lord,' quoted in Virion (1972), p.168.
21. 'Be the deputy of the King of Heaven who is the King of France.'
22. Virion (1972).
23. Virion (1972), p.182/83.
24. By Saint Remigius, Bishop of Reims in 496.
25. Rooyen (2014), personal communication.
26. 'The good quarrel of the kingdom of France.' Quoted in Virion (1972), p.69.
27. Quoted in Virion (1972), p.99.
28. Compare Masilius of Padua's *Defensor Pacis* (1324), an outright statement of the supremacy of the state (Tuchman, 1982, p.59).
29. Virion (1972), p.90.
30. Cf. Dunois.
31. Richey (2000), p.11 of 32 of a downloaded file.
32. Montgomery (1961), p.59.
33. Pernoud (1962), p.147. Freely translated.
34. Quoted in Fabre (1948, Dutch translation), p.15.
35. Cf. Thomas (2000) and Fabre (1948, Dutch translation), p.119.
36. Thomas (2000), p.308.
37. Thomas (2000), p.329.
38. Poortenaar (1949?), p.6, p.84.
39. Cf. the definition of strategy according to Clausewitz (1987).
40. Cf. Fabre (1948, English translation), p.233.
41. Cf. Fabre (1948, English translation), p.215 in conjunction with p.233.
42. Fabre (1948, English translation), p.236.
43. Without Jeanne, Europe would have been confronted much earlier with the darkness of religious and social revolutions, and the attempted unification of Europe without God. See Virion (1972), p.100/101.
44. And the reshaping of Europe by England and Burgundy – which had been stopped by Jeanne a century earlier – would have taken place. That would have involved a new, Anglo-Saxon economy-based Europe (similar to the EU). In such a Europe, the Pope of Rome is subordinated to anti-pontifical councils (in short, democracy in the Church). Virion, p.100, 136.
45. Virion (1972), p.100.
46. During the expansion of the Roman Empire they made the roads and newly conquered territories unsafe.
47. http://nl.wikipedia.org/wiki/Jacquerie, accessed 7 April 2014.
48. Quoted in Liddell Hart (1944), p.232.

49. Quoted in Holden (1991), p.11 of 15 of a downloaded file. See also Tuchman (1982).
50. Ibid.
51. Beaufre (1965), p.57.
52. Quoted in Holden (1991), p.11/12 of 15 of a downloaded file.
53. Pernoud & Clin (2011), p.64.
54. See note 106.
55. Rehabilitation, 05, p.3 of 9 of a downloaded file.
56. The use of Stukas by the Luftwaffe in the Second World War had the same purpose.
57. Mantel (1931).
58. Ibid.
59. See Mantel (1931), p.120/121. An attack is not without disadvantages, as much as there are pros and cons to defense – see Liddell Hart (1944), p.242: 'As when snow is squeezed into a snowball, direct pressure has always the tendency to harden and consolidate the resistance of an opponent – and the more compact it becomes the more difficult it is to melt.'
60. The aforementioned arguments in favour of attack are affirmed by the life and works of 'Lawrence of Arabia'. This man – in reality Colonel Thomas Edward Lawrence – is considered the master of the – by nature – offensive guerrilla. During the First World War he played a leading role in the Middle East in the struggle of the English against the Turks (then allies of Germany). In this battle the Arabs came to the side of the English. The Colonel managed to unite the Arab tribes by preaching to them a kind of 'crusade' against the Turks, their common enemy. Lawrence was admired by Liddell Hart, Churchill, and the Vietnamese general Giap.
61. Quoted (and roughly translated) in Connelly (2002), p.100.
62. Fabre (1948, English translation), p.231.
63. Sibley & Fry (2008), p.108.
64. Beaufre (1965), p.107. The indirect approach was Rommel's strong point: he usually attacked from an unexpected direction at an unexpected moment. Sibley & Fry (2008), p.109.
65. Beaufre (1965), p.107.
66. Continental powers mainly use the direct strategy. See the Schlieffen-Moltkeplan (= German attack plan in the First World War). Such a strategy is, however, catastrophic if the enemy has strong positions.
67. See Mantel (1931).
68. DeVries quoted in Taylor (2010), p.72.
69. Quoted in Connelly (2002), p.129. Incidentally, at Austerlitz, Napoleon also won through a frontal attack (on a limited front).
70. Creveld (2001), p.276.
71. La Charité-sur-Loire was the place where 'seigneur-brigand' Perrinet

Gressart had installed himself. This robber, who had ties with Philip the Good (Thomas, 2000, p.442), had once captured Trémoïlle to release him only against a high ransom. Jeanne had been instructed to attack this crook, a command which she had accepted. On the way to Charité-sur-Loire, Jeanne conquered Saint-Pierre-le-Moûtier, a town that was also in the hands of Gressart. It was during the siege of Saint-Pierre-le-Moûtier (November 1429) that Jean d'Aulon saw Jeanne with only four or five men left.

72. Old Testament: Ecclesiasticus ('Jesus Sirach') 3.26.
73. And no one, by the way, can explain her remarkable implicit knowledge of canon law and theology that she demonstrated during her trial in Rouen. See Taylor (2010), p.150. The same applies to her intuition regarding the essence of the feudal contract as manifested in her opinion on the relationship between God and king.
74. Taylor (2010), p.89.

15 ASPECTS OF JEANNE'S TACTICS

'But choice of tactics is in fact strategy.'
- General Beaufre

According to the German Field Marshal Helmuth von Moltke (1800-1891), chief of staff of the Prussian army for thirty years, 'no plan survives the first five minutes of the confrontation with the enemy'. And according to Basil Liddell Hart, captain and military historian, 'a plan that has no possibility of adaptation spells bankruptcy if it goes wrong'.[1] Therefore, there must be an extension of the strategy, a mode of thinking that, if necessary, adapts the general strategic guidelines in order to cope with unforeseen circumstances on the ground. Hence the importance of 'tactics', that is to say: an assembly of *manoeuvres* in line with the strategic design discounting unforeseen circumstances. These manoeuvres are about 'the use of resources based on *proceedings*' (see below) but never without an assessment of the actual situation. The 'use of resources' is about 'fire' and 'movement' with the aim of bringing friendly troops into a more advantageous position than the enemy units.[2]

The manoeuvre comprises – according to De Vos (2006) – of six elements:[3]

(a) The 'posture', i.e. the action form characterised by proceedings.

(b) The (tactical) 'objective', i.e. the material end goal of the manoeuvre.

(c) The entrance to the battlefield ('axis')

(d) The 'dispositive', i.e. the arrangement in the field.

(e) The 'deadlines', i.e. the start and end of the manoeuvre.

(f) The 'rhythm', i.e. the use of resources distributed in time and space.

I will now briefly relate these (basic) elements to Jeanne d'Arc.

(a): *The 'posture'*

There are *tactical* and *combat* proceedings.[4] The former deal with the way in which a unit, composed of sub-units of different 'weapons'[5], is deployed to carry out its mission. [For example, if the army is to slow down the enemy, the generals have two tactical proceedings: (1) the continuous battle 'in the depth', or (2) the temporary defence of a position.] A combat proceeding is the same as a tactical proceeding, but now the unit consists of a single 'weapon'.

The posture is indeed about proceedings, *but not only*.[6] According to Helmuth von Moltke[7], a commander must be able to make bold use of opportunities that arise – unexpectedly – in the implementation of the strategic setup.[8] In the same vein,

Liddell Hart writes: 'Most victories in history have been won by seizing opportunities offered by the loser.'[9] In short, one's own assessment of the situation is always an additional crucial element.

Rommel, for example, had a particular talent for spotting the tactical possibilities of a situation. He immediately saw opportunities when it became clear that the expedition to Greece deprived the British forces in North Africa of a large part of their strength.[10]

Jeanne also saw and exploited 'opportunities' where others wanted to stop, like at Orléans. Jeanne could identify unexpected opportunities; her performance at Meung testifies to this, but also her stellar management of the situation when Richemont suddenly arrived, threatening the unity of the entire enterprise. All this suggests that the French heroine was blessed with a *coup d'oeil*.

(b): *The 'objective'*

The (tactical) objective is always something concrete, like conquering a hill, granting support to advancing troops, or a barrage of artillery. Jeanne never lacked in concrete objectives. Of course, she thereby always encountered unforeseen difficulties. In order to be prepared for this 'friction', the Maid had to study the theatre of operations beforehand and in person. This 'reconnaissance' characterised Jeanne's conduct as much as her tactical attitude.[11] She gauged the depth of canals, explored positions and studied walls and bastions. The study of the theatre of operations is also necessary to intelligently line up the troops in the field (the 'dispositive', see below).

(c): The entrance to the battlefield ('axis')

Essential to the tactics of La Pucelle was that her mere presence concentrated most of the resources on the axis of a certain area. *For where Jeanne was, there was the fight.* In this way she led her troops at Orléans in successive, direct, frontal attacks: first in the attack of the militia at the bastion Saint-Loup, then in the attack on the siege tower at the convent of Saint-Augustine, and finally in the attack on the bastion of Les Tourelles. All these attacks were initiated (or revitalised) by La Pucelle.

Our heroine enforced a quick solution through short, fierce, frontal aggression. This preference stands out the more because in martial history most successes are achieved not by a direct approach, but by approaching the opponent in a geographically unexpected way, thus destabilising him before any attack actually takes place (the indirect approach).[12]

(d): *The 'dispositive'*

When arranging the troops in the field, Jeanne wanted to seize the enemy with superior force *at decisive points*. Thus the Maid wished to be sure – by a careful arrangement of her men – that she always had more men at the site where she sought the decision. But in addition, she certainly must have answered the question of whether a pike man should be arranged alongside a warrior with a battle weapon; or whether it was better to unite the pike men in the first ranks, and the men with battle weapons in the second ranks.[13] If her decisions would not have reflected military knowledge, then there would have been no reason to praise her for arranging the troops [a task which usually lasted two to three hours!][14]

(e): *The 'deadlines'*

Jeanne determined the beginning and the end of the manoeuvre in some decisive battles. This was the case when she intervened during the siege of the stronghold of Les Tourelles (Orléans) and the siege of Saint-Pierre-le-Moustier. In the first instance, she managed to stop the Bastard in his retreat and then initiated the decisive attack. In the second case, she revitalised an attack that – due to great opposition from the town – had already been abandoned.

Here we have the pertinent and detailed testimony of Jean d'Aulon. This squire was struck in the heel by an arrow. He limped along in the rear guard of the retreating troops. Suddenly he noticed that Jeanne had been isolated with a few men far behind the rest of the troops.[15] D'Aulon feared that she was exposing herself to danger, managed to get a horse and quickly rode to her. He asked what she was doing and why she did not – like the others – withdraw. Jeanne took off her helmet and replied that she was not alone, that she still had 50000 fighters with her, and that she would not go away before she had taken the city. She commanded: 'Everyone to the faggots and hurdles, to make the bridge!'[16] Then the fighters came from all sides, closed the moat and took the city without meeting much resistance.

During the rehabilitation process (1455-1456), Jean d'Aulon stated that Jeanne, whatever she may have said, did not have more than four or five men around her, and that he was sure of it, as were many others who had seen her in the same condition. Jean d'Aulon added that 'all the deeds of the Maid seemed to him to be more divine and miraculous than otherwise, and that it was not possible for so young a Maid to do such things without the Will and Guidance of Our Lord'.[17]

(f): *The 'rhythm'*

Jeanne's remarkable talent for the distribution of resources ('rhythm') was particularly evident in her use of artillery, a weapon that was then on the rise. The superior French artillery perhaps played the greatest role in the successes at Beaugency and Troyes. ['Le feu est tout,' Napoleon said a few centuries later.] The use of this weapon must be seen against the backdrop of a time when the defence of a city still consisted mainly of the agility of each defender using his own weapon.

Incidentally, Jeanne's use of artillery did not mean that she fired guns herself. At that time the operation of such a device was a hazardous affair. The men who were called to this task were hired specialists who also owned the apparatus. 'Gunners' formed an elite. These technicians, who were usually much older than the soldiers, were above all keen to save their precious cannons. Part of a commander's concern was therefore to have enough guards by each cannon so that the gunners stuck to their cannons when the situation became threatening for themselves and/or their guns. Here Jeanne's charisma probably inspired many gunners.

The main principle of the execution of the tactical operation is that it must be implemented quickly. 'No day, no hour may pass unused.'[18] The 'momentum' must be preserved. In addition, speed not only benefits the element of surprise, but also the morale.[19] Moreover, speed and surprise prevent the enemy taking countermeasures. The direct goal of speed (and strength and violence) is (a) the immobilisation or paralysis of the enemy, and (b) the creation of 'facts on the ground', whether or not as a basis for further negotiation.

Characteristic of Jeanne was the speed with which she thought and acted. For the one who attacks quickly (and stealthily), forces his plan on the other, restricts his freedom of action, and determines the beginning and the end of the manoeuvre. It was always the habit of the Maid to attack without delay, to confront the opponent head on. [Something the English failed to do on the first day of Rommel's offensive at Tobroek when they lost themselves in too slow, ineffective and disjointed responses.[20]]

The Desert Fox, like Jeanne, was a decisive individual. 'Speed of manoeuvre in operations and a quick response to the command are indispensable,' wrote Rommel. 'Troops must be able to carry out operations at top speed, while ensuring perfect coordination. To be content with a certain standard is fatal. One must continually strive for the best performance, because the party that makes a greater effort is faster, and the fastest wins the battle.'[21]

According to Pernoud & Clin (2011), 'speed' characterises Jeanne's every action;[22] when the king dawdled she became sad. For example, the time between Patay and the departure from Gien was too long for her taste; a total of 11 days. Jeanne could not stand it. Annoyed – and possibly to influence the king – she demonstratively sleeps next to her men in the open fields two days before the departure of the king.

In this context, the events at Jargeau are also illuminating. Jeanne wants to act quickly to not give the English time to catch their breath and prevent Fastolf and his men in Janville from uniting with Talbot, Suffolk and Scales. But d'Alençon does not see Jeanne's argument, upon which Jeanne is forced to sternly admonish him.

For Jeanne, tactics were largely a matter of speed.[23],[24]*Possibly, La Pucelle was obsessed with the idea that she had to act fast ('Je durerai un an, guère plus!'*[25]*). In any case, she realised all too well* *that she should not leave the English time to recover and reorganise.*[26] *Therefore, she carried out her attacks one after the other, as quickly as she could.*[27]

However, there is a downside to pace and speed. Penetrating fast and deep into enemy territory makes sense, but not so fast and so deep that your own safety is compromised, for example because your logistic network can no longer keep up. Exactly this lack of support became a problem for the French army when it took up position before the walls of Troyes. Due to the rapid advance, supplies were an issue. [Rommel learned the same lesson in France;[28] and Hitler would not fare better in Russia in 1941).[29]]. In some respects, the situation of Jeanne's army at Troyes was similar to that of Rommel's Africa Korps when it faced logistical problems as a result of its fast and deep advance into enemy territory.

Another problem of advancing in this manner is that the leader of the avant-garde is no longer in close contact with the rear guard. This was less of a problem in the time of Jeanne d'Arc because in those days the armies and the battlefield were much smaller, and warriors approached each other frontally in a close-knit formation; one still fought shoulder to shoulder. [This was possible and necessary because firearms had not yet been introduced and an isolated army unit had only limited means to resist.[30]]

After a successful attack, the tactician must consolidate and organise the defence of the captured terrain. This is precisely what the diplomats, after Reims, did not consider in their negotiations. Jeanne, on the other hand, sought to secure the Creil-Soissons line. [Here is an example to support this sensible idea: when the Americans invaded Iraq, the 101st Airborne Division oversaw the consolidation of conquered areas.[31]]

In the footsteps of d'Alençon, Stephen Richey praises Jeanne's tactics (and strategy): 'She especially honored the principles of maintenance of morale, objective, offensive, speed, maneuver, mass, and economy of force.'[32] *All this, I add, without training and without experience. But she was blessed with a wonderful coup d'oeil.*

It should be noted that Jeanne's frontal (= direct) tactical attacks mostly concerned *sieges*, that is: military situations with their own, specific circumstances. The focus when breaking a siege by storm is the overcoming of – raised – barriers, for example a palisade or a fortified wall with a canal around it; this without trivialising the danger that the enemy exploits this delay to implement a more cunning plan. The commander first has to face the problem of how to get the guns safely to the ramparts. The solution would only become clear centuries later (in the 17th century, with Vauban, 'the great military engineer of the reign of Louis XIV').[33]

The special thing about the situation at Orléans was that La Pucelle had to besiege the besiegers. But contrary to what tradition prescribed – namely to surround the English over a broad front and force them to surrender (for example through starvation) – Jeanne led her troops into successive, direct, frontal attacks (with Les Tourelles as the final point of engagement).[34] These attacks lasted long, were brutal and had many casualties.[35] Jeanne's men were aware of that. But nevertheless, writes Emilie Roberts (2011), 'the soldiers followed Jeanne d'Arc into battle and they continued to wage that battle for over twelve [!] hours, despite heavy losses and witnessing their champion being struck by an enemy arrow. The taking of Les Tourelles was an event that required men who had something in their minds and hearts for which the word 'morale' seems too small to describe.'[36]

Thanks to Jeanne's victory at Orléans – and later victories – many cannons fell into French hands. Jeanne subsequently maximised the strategic deployment of those cannons. 'Jargeau was bombarded for a day and a night before the city was stormed; and the heavily fortified castle of Beaugency was forced to surrender by a bombardment so that an infantry attack on the walls of the city was no longer needed.'[37] 'Troyes, the city in which the hated treaty was drawn that the French kingdom was bequeathed to the heirs of Henry V, resisted the royalist French until the moment the inhabitants saw La Pucelle prepare for a bombardment by artillery – at which the city immediately capitulated.'[38] *Thanks to Jeanne the Dauphin's army finally carried out a successful 'modern war'.*[39] When the infantry was not needed, losses would correspondingly decrease (with associated consequences for Jeanne's fame). The new weapons and the new strategy were an important element of the great success of the Loire offensive.[40]

---

1. Liddell Hart (1944), p.245.
2. For a full explanation of tactics, see De Vos (2006).
3. De Vos (2006).
4. Ibid.
5. One needs to differentiate between the following 'weapons': infantry, armoured troops, artillery, genius, logistics, transmission troops and administration.
6. Proceedings must have existed in the time of Jeanne. How else could her fellow commanders speak about her expertise?
7. Moltke was the designer of a system used to manage large armies.
8. This was the policy of the Wehrmacht during the Second World War. All commanders were presented with their assignments in this specific form. This was in contrast to the attitude in the American and British armies where everyone was kept on a short leash. Rooyen (2014), personal communication.
9. Liddell Hart (1944), p.272.

10. Sibley & Fry (2008), p.89.
11. Napoleon and Sherman (an American general in the Civil War) were also renowned for their reconnaissance work.
12. De Vos (2006), Beaufre (1965), p.107 et sequens. According to Liddell Hart (1944), the direct approach is the usual strategy. [Although it is not the most successful!]
13. DeVries, p.129.
14. Ibid.
15. Fabre (1948, Dutch translation), p.212.
16. Rehabilitation, o3, p.7 of 9 of a downloaded file.
17. Ibid.
18. Mantel (1931), p.131.
19. The satellites of today make 'surprise' much harder.
20. Sibley & Fry (2008), p.131.
21. Sibley & Fry (2008), p.138.
22. Pernoud & Clin (2011), p.94.
23. DeVries (2011), p.92.
24. Pernoud & Clin (2011), p.94.
25. 'I will stay with you for a year, barely any longer.'
26. Richey, quoted in Taylor (2010), p. 90/91.
27. Ibid.
28. But he would repeat his error in North Africa.
29. Rees (2013), p.252.
30. Beaufre (1965), p.59.
31. De Vos (2006), p.107.
32. Richey quoted in Taylor (2010), p.72.
33. Earl (1960), p. 33. Vauban came up with the following: Dig your way to the ramparts via parallel slots (this was often done at night). The first parallel slot surrounded the fortress. From there, the besiegers dug zigzagging trenches to the fortress. A second parallel slot (+ 'approaching trenches') followed and finally the besiegers completed a third parallel slot at the foot of the fort's wall. When the work was finished, artillery was brought on-site. While the artillery fired, a tunnel was dug.
34. Cf. Roberts (2011), p.12 of 41 of a downloaded file.
35. Cf. Roberts (2011), p.14 of 41 of a downloaded file.
36. Ibid.
37. Roberts (2011), p.39 of 41 of a downloaded file.
38. Ibid.
39. Ibid.
40. Roberts (2011), p.40 of 41 of a downloaded file.

16 JEANNE'S POWER

'One obtains better results with a soft word
and an army than with only a soft word.'
- A. Capone

Yukl (1998) distinguishes, based on extensive meta-research, the following types of power:[1] (1) power based on one's position ('positional power'), (2) personal power, and (3) political power. I will now briefly relate these to Jeanne d'Arc.

(1): *Positional power*

With 'positional power', Yukl (1998) means the possibilities available to someone purely and solely based on his position in an organisation. First, think of a person's *formal* authority, that is, the authority that is legally due to someone on the basis of his appointment. This kind of authority certainly played a role in the present topic of discussion, for, after all, Jeanne called herself in her letter to the English 'chef de guerre' and such an indication obviously has an effect, even if the term was the work of the executive writer of that letter. Certain is that Jeanne was appointed *commander* and that she had a corresponding entourage. As a result, La Pucelle was able to influence (through her arrangements of the artillery and her fighters) the physical environment, and thus the behaviour of the opponent. Jeanne did this at Troyes. The result was that the city surrendered without a blow or shot.

Even though Jeanne had some formal power, this power was much less important than her *exceptional character* and her *impressive eloquence*. These attributes were even more significant because an 'army' at that time was not a monolithic, strict hierarchy, but a rather informal power structure. In such a loose weave, strength of personality counts much more than appointed rank. Other factors also contributed to the Maid's positional power, for example her management of what we now call 'Human Resources'. It was Jeanne – and no other – who, as a magnet, attracted people to serve in the French army.

Stephen Richey (2000) expresses it like this: 'Clearly, Jeanne d'Arc's moral inspiration turned an army of sullen professional mercenaries into a cross-social class army of crusaders.'[2] *Nothing could be truer.* Jeanne d'Arc was the first to spread the idea of a nation that common people could experience as theirs and fight for. On this essential point I quote Alain Chartier (1385–1430), poet and political writer: '[Jeanne d'Arc] a haussé les esprits vers l'espérance des temps meilleurs.'[3] This statement was supported by several other writings at the time (e.g. Christine de Pisan's *La ditié de Jeanne d'Arc*[4]). Furthermore, many letters about the mystical visionary circulated, including one from the nobleman Guy de Laval (quoted by Pernoud in her *Jeanne d'Arc par elle-même et par ses témoins*). This letter documents how excited Guy and his brother were about Jeanne.[5] They were not the only ones. Even Bedford was impressed by the Maid, although he accused her of sorcery and witchcraft in a letter to his king.

In short, France was thrown into a frenzy due to Jeanne La Pucelle's victories. The people were willing to follow her to the end of the world. The army was over the moon. It obeyed her because it wanted to. It was therefore no more than natural that, as a result, Jeanne had the power to 'reward' or 'punish' her people, another significant facet of positional power. To be with her was in itself a reward for the fighters given that Jeanne was the object of their sublimated love. They considered it a 'punishment' when the Maid threatened to leave the army if the soldiers and officers did not quit swearing. And if someone so much as thought of not obeying Jeanne in terms of manners and moral behaviour, she did not hesitate to threaten them with her sword.[6]

A CEO of an organisation is normally provided with solid information. But in the Maid's case she herself had to search for information. At Orléans (the ceasefire) and during the journey that brought her to the walls of Paris (the negotiations with the Duke of Burgundy), Jeanne was even *denied* information! The inadequate provision of information indicates the diverging intentions of the court with its intrigues and the men in the field.

The importance of information was rubbed in the face of Rommel, an experienced general, at Alamein (November 1942) when his offensive towards the Suez Canal was halted and his opponent Montgomery decided to attack for a second time. [The first attack had failed.] Rommel had organised his impressive defence without enough reconnaissance. He was thus labouring under the misapprehension that the British would put in their main effort along the coast. Consequently, Rommel had the coastal flank strengthened, at the expense of the centre, where Montgomery attacked. The evening after, following a bloody battle, the German-Italian front collapsed and a great pursuit began.[7]

(2): *Personal power*

The heroine of Orléans managed to eliminate the divisions between the commanders on account of her personal attributes. This was crucial in the success of the French army.

In the analysis of this type of power, the 'attributes of the agent' and the 'agent-target relationship' play decisive roles. Specific elements in this analysis are (a) expertise, (b) friendship & loyalty, and (c) charisma.

(a) Expertise

Expertise is highly credible if *demonstrated*. Jeanne did so, until Paris. She simply delivered. This impressed the people around her, then the whole army, and finally – by means of social contagion – the French population as a whole.

It was especially during the preparations for the besieging of Troyes that the peasant girl from Domrémy – who had been given (or taken?) the leadership – demonstrated her expertise and managerial talent. According to the Bastard, she placed the tents directly along the canal around Troyes and performed 'many miraculous manoeuvres which had not been thought of by two or three accomplished generals working together.'[8] [In terms of tactics: Jeanne concerned herself with 'the dispositive of the army in the field'.] She also deployed field artillery and heavy siege equipment judiciously. The French saint ordered her men to aim the latter at the corners of square castle towers, but at the centre of round towers.[9] [The firing of a cannon was tricky at the time; in addition, the besieged also had cannons and obviously did not allow any gun ports to be directed at them.]

It was also La Pucelle who gave the order to cross the canal using bundles of twigs and branches and to begin the attack.

The aforementioned remark from the Bastard is confirmed by the testimony of Dunois: 'And so well did [Jeanne] work during the night, that, the next day, the Bishop (Jean Leguise, ennobled by Charles VII for his share in the surrender of the town) and the citizens came all trembling to place their submission in the King's hands. Afterwards, it was known that, at the very moment Jeanne told the king's Council not to pass by the town, the inhabitants had sudden lost heart, and had occupied themselves only in seeking refuge in the churches.'[10]

At this point, I would like to draw attention to the successive testimonies of Simon Chartres, Thibault d'Armagnac and d'Alençon:[11]

* Simon Chartres (President of the Chamber of Accounts to Dauphin and King Charles VII) who accompanied Jeanne's army in the field):

'Jeanne was very simple in all her actions, except in the conduct of war, in which she was altogether an expert.'

* Thibauld d'Armagnac, knight, bailli de Chartres:

'[In] the leading and drawing up of armies and in the conduct of war, in disposing an army for battle and haranguing the soldiers, she behaved like the most experienced captain in all the world, like one with a whole lifetime of experience.'

* D'Alençon:

'In everything that she did, apart from the conduct of the war, Jeanne was young and simple; but in the conduct of war she was most skillful, both in carrying a lance herself, in drawing up the

army in battle order, and in placing the artillery. And everyone was astonished that she acted with such prudence and clear-sightedness in military matters, as cleverly as some great captain with twenty- or thirty-years' experience; and especially in the placing of artillery, for in that she acquitted herself magnificently.'

'Prudentia' (the virtue of caution) can easily be translated into 'practical wisdom'. It can be defined as 'doing the right thing given what the actor anticipates'. No virtuous deed can be truly accomplished unless directed by caution, 'the charioteer of the virtues'. Prudentia is highly relevant to making difficult choices; it allows us to see which specific means (for example a medical treatment) is proportional to a certain goal (like healing). Prudentia also enables us to find the right balance between extremes, for example cowardice and overconfidence.[12]

Prudentia can only exist if one possesses other virtues and focuses on the purpose of life. Practically speaking, prudentia is a question of: (1) deliberating (followed by making a choice) and (2) commanding, i.e. making use of the means by which a goal is achieved (execution). When choosing and recommending, the mind plays a dominant role; it directs and organises and it suggests the will (which only 'pushes') the right means. Practising the virtue of the prudentia protects the actor from 'jumping to conclusions', levity, and indecision.[13]

The prudence of the Maid of Orléans cannot possibly be attributed to long-term experience. Jeanne did not have military experience, certainly not when she appeared before the gates of Orléans. Therefore, the acts of the girl from Domrémy cannot be traced back to some form of 'case based reasoning'. Neither do I believe that Jeanne's thinking found support in a system of structurally dealing with uncertainty, for example by – possibly unconsciously – thinking in opportunities and useful outcomes.

Through such thinking one can never achieve the speed and certainty of Jeanne's decisions. [A good decision that comes in an hour late is equivalent to 'no decision'.]

I therefore read in Jeanne a *certainty* that – coupled with her intuitive *knowing* – can only be explained by a supernatural element. No one writing about Jeanne d'Arc can ignore her fairly exact predictions that all – although not all within her lifetime – came true. I am thinking about the sword that was found at Fierbois, the estimation of the time she needed to liberate Orléans and especially her prediction concerning the duration of her own mission: 'un an, guère plus.'[14] Jeanne knew with certainty things that ordinary people cannot know. The latter can only resort to calculations based on subjective *probabilities*. But without formal support and good data, subjective probability estimates usually lead to bias, 'lucky outcomes' and irrelevance.

Incidentally, the more reaching the target relies on expertise, the greater the power of the expert leader. Sometimes the expert does not live up to his reputation for expertise. [Like Jeanne's failure in front of the walls of Paris, at least in the perception of the court and the clique of advisors surrounding the king]. That is the end of his power.

(b) Friendship & loyalty ('referent power')

Let us study the testimony of Perceval de Gagny, chronicler of d'Alençon: 'And although the King had no money to pay his army, all his knights, squires, soldiers and ordinary people were willing to serve him on that journey [to Reims] in the company of the Maid; they said they would follow Jeanne anywhere.'[15] The loyalty to Jeanne thus carried immense power. Indeed, her soldiers and collaborators (d'Alençon, La Hire, Dunois) were extremely loyal. In the literature one finds that such a thing is strongest in cases of personal identification. [In such a form of identification, the 'target' – out of need for acceptance and esteem from its leader – tries to adopt the attitudes and behaviours of the leader; of course this takes time but this time span can be shortened by consideration and friendliness on the part of the leader.]

Referent power, finally, promotes commitment, possibly including the blind carrying out of orders from the leader, even if they are criminal in nature as in the case of Hitler or the infamous Manson murders in the late 1960s.[16]

(c) Charisma

Sometimes followers experience such an intense attraction that it seems as if the leader possesses an extraordinary quality called 'charisma'. Is charisma nothing but personal power? Or does charisma exist in 'something' that followers attribute to the leader, whether or not as a result of mutual influence? For further commentary on Jeanne's charisma, see Chapter 19.

(3): *Political power*

Political power is about having control over decisions and forming coalitions. Jeanne had this political power not on formal grounds but based on (a) her great personal strength, (b) the essentially political nature of her mission, and (c) the devotion of her army.

DeVries (2011) writes: 'She fought for command of the lacklustre French military leaders, and she received it. She fought for the allegiance of the French soldiers, and she earned it. She fought for the love of the inhabitants of [Orléans], and she gained it.'[17] When one has won the allegiance and the love of the army and the people, then to me one has power in the political sense.

---

1. See Yukl (1998).
2. Richey (2000), p.7 of 32 of a downloaded file.
3. Pernoud (1962), p.129, quoting a letter. Freely translated: 'She has cheered up the people so that they have found hope again that things will improve.'
4. Translation: *The Poem of Joan of Arc*.
5. Pernoud (1962), p.130.
6. Taylor (2010), p.89 (quoting Ayroles).
7. See De Vos (2006), p.81/82.
8. Ibid.
9. Defenders built round towers 'for better flanking fire' (Newman, 1942, p.121); it was the latest news in the construction of fortresses, brought from the East by the Crusaders.
10. Rehabilitation, o6, p.4 of 9. Also quoted in Pernoud (1962), p.144. See also Richey (2000), p.12 of 52 of a downloaded file. The words of the Bastard have also been confirmed by Simon Charles, court bureaucrat, who witnessed the event.
11. Quoted in Richey (2000), p.6 of 32 of a downloaded file. See also Rehabilitation.
12. Between cowardice and overconfidence is 'courage'.
13. A prudent person also shuns – in a certain way and conditionally – 'the wisdom of the world which ignores God'. In this regard, it should be noted that the message of the parable of the unjust steward is not about justice, but about 'understanding'.
14. 'A year, barely more.'
15. Pernoud (1962), p.141. Freely translated.
16. Charles Manson was the charismatic leader of a 'family' of predominantly young female followers. The 'family' was responsible for seven murders including that of the pregnant actress Sharon Tate (the wife of film director Roman Polanski).
17. DeVries (2011), p.90.

17 HOW DID JEANNE OBTAIN POWER?

'I bore most willingly
that which had been ordained for me by our Lord;
and, meanwhile,
in all I waited upon our Lord.'
- Jeanne d'Arc

In *sociological explanations*, power in a group is obtained by 'social processes' in which the leader and his followers mutually influence each other. The leader demonstrates or projects therein status, 'good judgement', and success in achieving goals.[1] Jeanne d'Arc mastered this.

In *'actor-oriented theories'*, the leader is in the spotlight as a unique, indispensable and irreplaceable *troubleshooter*; he undertakes political manoeuvres (e.g. 'coalition formation', 'control over key decisions' and the like). Once in power, he effectuates situations through various influencing tactics. In the case of our saint, this happened not so much through a rational persuasive discourse, but in the unfolding of a coherent, clear, attractive vision that appealed to emotion and shared values, in particular patriotism.

Secondarily, Jeanne herself employed a *'legitimating tactic/strategy'*, that is: she referred to the fact – by means of a written document, namely her letter to the English – that a superior (the king), had legitimately appointed her commander ('I am Commander'). Admittedly, the Maid of Orléans denied in her trial that she referred to herself as 'chef de guerre'. It is possible that this is an insertion by the scribe to whom Jeanne dictated her letter[2] but the effect was the same.

In a way, the Maid of Orléans also used the so-called *'coalition strategy'* – against Trémoïlle and Regnault de Chartres. She did this through her association with La Hire, Dunois, de Xaintrailles, and her closest fellow warrior d'Alençon.

Furthermore, the reader should keep in mind that the village girl from Domrémy was – from Vaucouleurs on – surrounded by a radiating aura,[3] the aura of a saint. To conclude this consideration of the 'actor-oriented theories', let us not forget the 'titillating effect' that female warriors have on men.[4] One needs only to consider the nickname that Jeanne chose for herself (that Marina Gordon (2001) found 'teasing').[5]

Situational factors that played a role in the success of Jeanne d'Arc

No one operates in a vacuum; the Maid acted in a context. There was the political crisis, there was fear, and daily life was disrupted. Furthermore, defeatism and apathy caused an acute need for assertive leaders, that is to say: persuasive captains who promise clear, challenging goals and who give fighters confidence because they are decisive and unshakable in their actions. But at the time leaders like that were nowhere to be found. This was all the more deplorable because in tumultuous times, decisiveness is all that counts (politics and governance become influential during a more stable phase).

A significant factor in the success of the French heroine was the credence that many gave to the prophesy of the legendary Merlin that a maid from Lorraine would save France in her most fearful hour. Charles VII himself had had his own experience with Marie d'Avignon, the prophetess who had foretold that a virgin would take up weapons and liberate France. Finally there was, of course, the fact that Jeanne's *Letter to the English* was followed by an astonishing success!

Besides all this, La Pucelle probably had nothing to do with the complex logistics of an advancing army; the details of it were certainly the responsibility of her fellow commanders. [I am talking about the establishment (and guarding) of operation lines, the transport of heavy siege vehicles, issues relating to 'guns and butter', financial arrangements, administrative tasks, and all sorts of 'friction' that is associated with an advancing army.[6]] For instance, after Jargeau Jeanne wanted to go directly to Meung. However, logistics-wise this was not possible because the guns that had proved so successful had to be shipped to Meung-sur-Loire and the army had to reorganise itself.

As the Maid of Orléans did not have to deal with logistics, she was able to concentrate on her leadership. She must nevertheless have had a good intuition for logistics and topography (or at least a good disposition for appreciating situations from that point of view) for how else could she have become an extremely successful commander?

The Maid of Orléans also did not have to deal with the old generation of incompetent military leaders. Instead, she worked with a new generation of fresh young men, figures like d'Alençon, Dunois, La Hire, and De Xaintrailles. These men understood that something had to change to keep France afloat. 'Joan's moral inspiration, force of will, and...pragmatic drive to do what worked were the catalyst these men needed to make their efforts attain their fullest effect.'[7]

In addition to the above, the loose structure of the French army worked in Jeanne's favour, as previously discussed. Furthermore, the different parts of the army were less intertwined than nowadays: units of the Dauphinist army operated relatively independently of each other and were less dependent on cooperation. This last circumstance implies that a leader then was much less burdened with typical management- and network activities than his colleague today. 'In a system such as that, forceful eloquence and a strong character counted for more in Councils of War than formal factors of rank and position.'[8] [Structured military organisations make their debut only in the second half of the 18th century.[9]] Also, the armies were not so large (usually only several thousand men) and they had fewer *moving* parts. Because of the last factor alone, a medieval army was much less complex than a modern army.[10] One still fought shoulder to shoulder on a small battlefield and there was more room for individual initiative. In this context, Jeanne was able to manifest herself, instantaneously and perceptibly, to the entire army during a struggle.

Finally, the English had certainly underestimated the French at Orléans. They had not completely surrounded the city but spread their men over various forts. Even with the arrival of La Pucelle, they never seriously considered the possibility of the French coming out to engage the English in battle.

With her style of leadership, La Pucelle had a great impact.[11]

Today, such a thing is no longer possible; generals are more like managing directors of a department store.[12]

---

1. Other elements that Yukl (1998) mentions are loyalty to the group and input of innovative ideas for the purpose of the group goal.
2. Warner (2000), p.68.
3. Pernoud & Clin (2011), p.53.
4. Creveld (2001), p.121.
5. Gordon (2001).
6. Fabre (1948, Dutch translation), p.158; Mantle (1931), p.140 et sequens; DeVries (2011), p.133.
7. Richey (2000), p.21 of 32 of a downloaded file.
8. Richey (2000), p.17 of 32 of a downloaded file.
9. De Vos (2006), p.23.
10. This complexity carries the danger of increasing 'friction' and confusion.
11. See also Richey (2000), p.20 of 32 of a downloaded file.
12. Liddell Hart (1944), p.220.

18 HOW DID JEANNE LOSE POWER?

> 'For gold is tested in the fire,
> and the chosen in the furnace of humiliation.'
> - Ecclesiasticus ('Jesus Sirach') 2, 5

War, according to Clausewitz, is 'an act of violence driven to its limits'. All wars, he writes, resemble each other in this respect. On this 'ideal' (in a philosophical sense), 'modifications' are superimposed – by Clausewitz summarised as 'friction'. One such modification is the connection between war and politics. In relation to this relationship, Clausewitz observes that politics becomes important when the participants enter a more stable phase. At exactly such a point in our story, when Jeanne's mission was *seemingly* accomplished with the coronation of the king, the Maid of Orléans hit trouble. It was scheming politicians who caused her downfall. In the wake of these characters followed the defeatists who accused the great saint of being an unchristian warmonger who opposed peace treaties and armistices.[1,2]

In fact, as soon as Jeanne met with success, politicians at the court of Charles VII plotted against her because they did not believe in the divinity of her mission. Or perhaps it was because her military methods irked them. Especially Georges de la Trémoïlle, adviser to the king, was strongly opposed to the Maid, probably due to a combination of jealousy and a 'preference for diplomacy over struggle'. He was particularly opposed to Jeanne's fast-tracking the crowning and anointing of the Dauphin.

Trémoille was not happy that the Maid was so popular with the masses.[3] Archbishop Regnault the Chartres was equally concerned that Jeanne – especially in tandem with d'Alençon – posed a threat to his position. For this reason, the archbishop was in favour of maintaining the status quo, especially if it could benefit his own financial position.[4] Finally, the king himself was unreliable, suspicious and jealous, traits that meant that few kept their position by his side for long (which would eventually lead to great dissatisfaction, even rebellion).[5] In short, on one side we have the visionary heroine who wants the king, as a sovereign, to reach a peace where Philip submits to becoming a vassal. On the other side we have Trémoille and Regnault the Chartres who see the king and the duke as equals and who do not want to entertain a peace imposed by the king, but 'a peace in which the vassal has agreed. And that at the expense of thousands of concessions.'[6]

At the same time, King Charles – once crowned and stunned by the acclamations of the masses – was all too eager to listen to the advice of his diplomacy-oriented advisors.[7] While Jeanne and her associates had lobbied for a serious attempt to reclaim the whole of France, Trémoïlle and Regnault de Chartres advised the king to slow down and to conclude peace with the Duke of

Burgundy. Thus it was that Jeanne and her army were slipping into an engagement in which they not only fought the English, but also the apathy of their monarch.[8] An apathy that eventually led to increasing attacks from the Burgundians and Englishmen on recently liberated areas, at great cost; the reconquests by the English took more French lives than all the Maid's interventions by force combined. Stephen Richey (2000) even goes so far as to claim that 'Charles and the soft nobles of his court could easily come to see Jeanne, and the excessive patriotism of the masses devoted to her, as a greater threat than the English.'[9] It may indeed have been that Charles VII, after his coronation, conspired with his dubious advisers to stop La Pucelle in her tracks.[10]

Another example of politics prevailing over a military solution occurred during the final stage of the Vietnam war. At that point, American politics did not allow the war to be decided by military means, something that might have been achieved if the war had been fought by the US at a more intensive level. The price that the Americans paid for the primacy of politics was the compromised morale of the American armed forces for two decades.

As long as Jeanne celebrated triumphs, others succeeded in taking the place of Trémoïlle as the king's favourite. But when the Maid was severely injured before the walls of Paris, Trémoïlle returned as chief adviser with even more influence than before.[11] Suddenly Jeanne no longer seemed indispensable.[12]

Warner (2000) expresses the same thing in this way: 'Her traditional, honored form of heroics was useful; but once the Duke of Burgundy had come to the conference table, as he did for the Edict of Compiègne...there was no further use for a fire-eater like Jeanne.'[13] Jeanne's failure before the walls of Paris blemished the divinity of her mission. In the eyes of the court, that is!

The conflict between Jeanne and the scheming Trémoïlle can be traced back to a profound difference in their vision of war. For Trémoïlle, war was the continuation of politics, thus a rational instrument in the struggle for power. In this sense, La Trémoïlle – with Charles VII – was a precursor to Machiavelli and Clausewitz, though Trémoïlle understated the political effect of the deployment of the military. [This was quite different to Napoleon, who was also a great diplomat![14]] For La fille de Dieu, the war was *eschatological*. After all, her war was a holy war, a war to establish the hegemony of God in the world. This eschatological struggle even included a *cataclysmic* element because the Maid wanted to end the tragedy that had hit France, namely the invasion of the English.[15]

The study of the relationship between politics and military power is a classic subject. The reality is simply that *politicians* and *battle commanders* are rivals when it comes to influencing the goals and objectives of a strategy. Kissinger, the former Secretary of State of the US, believes that politicians and soldiers must cooperate.[16] But such an idea is quite problematic in itself, especially given that political advisors are usually (a) academic specialists who – organised in think tanks – are part of the military and industrial complex; or (b) lawyers and human rights activists (ideological proponents of soft power). These specialists thus impose too great an emphasis on either 'ideologically based aggression' or 'pacifism' at the expense of military expertise.[17]

Jeanne d'Arc's declining popularity soon had consequences. She was given a small army unit and only insignificant tasks. In addition, she was assigned to missions that required an offensive attitude for which her army was not equipped. She could not conquer La Charité-sur-Loire because she lacked the resources. In Rouen, Jeanne was asked why she hadn't taken La Charité when God had commanded her to do so. She answered: 'Who said to you that I had a commandment from God to do so.'[18]

The first months of 1430 forced the Maid into passivity (which she hated). Powerless, she had to witness how the Burgundians carried out attacks on territory that she had conquered a few months before;[19] and how the English and Burgundians were getting closer. This continued until Jeanne – on her own initiative and without saying goodbye to the king [which did not do her well] – undertook the trek to the endangered Compiègne in March 1430 to eventually fall into the hands of the Burgundians.

Jeanne's demise was due to the jealousy of the circle at court, an envy that was part of the greater problem of the relationship between military and political goals. In addition, this court cabal saw its (short term) interests seriously threatened by Jeanne.

---

1. Virion (1972), p.67.
2. One could make an analogy here with the German General Staff in the Second World War who refused to prioritise securing supplies for Rommel. See Sibley & Fry (2008), p.159.
3. Cf. Richey (2000), p.7 of 32 of a downloaded file.
4. Fabre (1948, Dutch translation), p.188. See also Virion (1972), p.65/66.
5. Pernoud & Clin (2011), p.126.
6. Fabre (1948, Dutch translation), p.189.
7. DeVries (2011), p.141.
8. Ibid.
9. Cf. Edward A. Lucie-Smith, quoted in Richey (2000), p.7 of 32 of a downloaded file.
10. A somewhat similar situation in which a successful military campaign was sacrificed to other goals is the case of General O'Connor, commander of the

Western Desert Force. On 9 December 1940 he launched an offensive against the Italians in Cyrenaica (North Africa). O'Connor was brilliant; the Allies were at the gates of Tripolitania and the Italians did not doubt that within a few days O'Connor would enter Tripoli. But the Allied commander was not given the opportunity because, on orders from headquarters, the offensive had to be stopped in order to move three divisions of veterans and an armoured brigade to Greece. Sibley & Fry (2008), p.83/84.
11. Charles VII possibly believed not so much in the Maid as in the miraculously found sword of Fierbois. In Jeanne's shattering of this sword the king saw an inauspicious sign.
12. Cf. Fabre (1948, Dutch translation), p.190.
13. Warner (2000), p.180.
14. Nester (2012).
15. See Rapoport's introduction to Clausewitz's *On War* (1987).
16. Baylis (1975).
17. Interview by Vrijsen, E., 'Safety expert: Western Europe lives in a fantasy,' https://www.elsevierweekblad.nl/buitenland/news/2014/08/veiligheidsexpert-west-europa-leeft-in-fantasie-1579185W, accessed 24 October 2019.
18. DeVries (2011), p.158.
19. Cf. DeVries (2011), p.161.

19 JEANNE AS A LEADER

'In battle man needs some rock to which to hold fast –
the artilleryman has his gun,
the airman his aeroplane,
infantry its group leader.'
- Basil Liddell Hart

According to Montgomery, a real leader possesses the ability and the will to unite men and women towards a common goal.[1] No one supports going to war if it is unclear what is intended and how it is going to be achieved.[2] It is the task of the leader to set the hearts of his followers ablaze. Consequently, a real leader manages to persuade others to trust and follow him. Jeanne d'Arc excelled in this area. She was a born leader. Her soldiers trusted her, even loved her, some until long after her death. In addition, she was both task and relationship oriented. The latter alone made her a great leader.

Jeanne had an impressive self-confidence, brought about by a sense of urgency, and was emotionally developed and stable (but not without empathy and a temper). She was honest, lived according to the values she proclaimed and could predict the future to a great extent. All the main characteristics and abilities of a leader were thus united in the Maid.

In addition, she was:

- *decisive* (like when Jeanne went against d'Alençon when he doubted the sense of the attack on Jargeau: 'Don't be afraid; the moment is favorable when it pleases God.'[3])
- *dominant* (the girl genius had a hold over Charles VII and the military commanders until Reims)
- *energetic* (during her short life, the Maid travelled 5000 km on horseback)
- *responsibility-accepting*, even if that meant that Jeanne had to bypass her superiors. (She ignored, for instance, the pause in fighting decided upon by the commanders at Orléans.)

The latter is comparable to the conduct of Rommel when he was formally placed under Italian supreme command in North Africa. Rommel formulated his disobedience as follows: 'I had decided – in view of the critical situation and the laziness of the Italian supreme command – to deviate from my instructions that I had to confine myself to explorations, and to take the command on the front as soon as possible in my own hands – at the latest after the arrival of the first German troops.'[4]

Even under great stress Jeanne kept her cool. This ability is especially important in military leaders given that most soldiers in combat situations rely on 'drills' or – through shell shock – cannot act at all. The quick and sure-fire intelligence of our heroine manifested itself also during the questioning by the Rouen judges; she embarrassed them time and time again with her quick-wittedness (plus her remarkable memory). That was the reason the chief judge[5] conducted matters behind closed doors for a while. Jeanne's ability 'to think quickly and creatively under conditions of horrific stress is [by all means] essential in a successful leader of forces in battle.'[6]

She also demonstrated:

- A 'socialized will to win'. La Pucelle surely wanted to 'win' at all times. But her power was entirely in the service of France. She did not ask for things for herself, except for a tax exemption for her native village and adjacent Greux. Incidentally, a strong desire to win is not decisive. Hitler also wanted to win no matter what. But he overestimated his own abilities, especially pertaining to his knowledge and experience in strategic matters. Intuition is not enough, at least not without divine guidance.
- A disregard for 'affiliation' (= wanting to be liked by others). The Maid told everyone the truth.[7] Even in chains and fevered, she could still explode in holy indignation about the activities of the infamous tribunal that would condemn her to the stake.[8]
- An inner conviction that her life depended more on her own actions than on chance or fate.[9] This explains why such 'internals' take on more responsibility and are proactive and forward-looking. They *learn* from setbacks instead of blaming 'bad luck'. [All this is done with self-confidence, creativity, flexibility and readiness to adapt.] The following statement by Jeanne is renowned in this respect: 'God helps those who help

themselves.' These words she spoke to d'Alençon at Jargeau when he was reluctant to act quickly.

Stephen Richey (2000) claims that Jeanne's talent to express forcefully 'that God was on the side of the French, but that the French themselves by their deeds had to earn God's help' was one of the characteristics that gathered a whole army behind her. Even at the stake the Maid of Orléans assumed responsibility. She acquitted everyone, including the king, a few minutes before her death. Earlier, at the cemetery of the abbey of Saint-Ouen (in Rouen) – where the Maid had her death sentence read and where she signed the 'abjuration statement' which she would later revoke – she stated that she did not blame anyone for her words and deeds, 'neither the King nor anyone else'. If these words and deeds are insufficient, she continued, 'in any way whatsoever', then it is 'me and no one else who is to blame'.[10]

This pure and brave girl demonstrated her competencies without ever becoming selfish or self-centred. She was never considered cynical or a bully. [Cynicism is never forgiven while a bully (like General Patton) gets away with his vice!] Jeanne paired all of this with interpersonal skills, persuasion and eloquence. And it did not stop there, because our heroine, as we have seen, was first-rate when it came to military strategic and tactical matters. In the field she was a fast problem solver. She had the 'intellectual flexibility' to quickly see the possibilities of a situation and to respond to it.[11] DeVries has another way of expressing the same thing: Jeanne, he said, 'was tactically capable enough to recognize an advantage when she saw one.'[12] Such a practical talent for problem solving is obviously an important feature for every manager, especially on the battlefield.[13] La Pucelle demonstrated this gift at Meung where, due to her swift action, Talbot and Scales could not unite with the troops of Fastolf.

Sometimes the Maid *miraculously* brought light to the darkness. For example, this was the case at Orléans when the transport of the equipment was hampered by the unfavourable direction of the wind. This problem did not disturb the Maid in any way. And whether she exploited a meteorological coincidence (the wind changed), or she had gifts of para- or supernatural order, she showed no trace of panic and chose the best option. In short, Jeanne d'Arc was an excellent thinker and doer. She was familiar with the art of leadership that demands firstly that the commander does not become seized by doubt.

All these characteristics and skills, wonderfully united in one person, made the Maid of Orléans a phenomenal motivator. Especially her certainty and calm were fully convincing. Before Reims, she did not know any unsteadiness in her military performance, that is to say moments when courage leaves a human being and a natural prudence turns to gloominess and despair, moments in which it is difficult to encourage men to put their lives at stake.[14] Undoubtedly, Charles VII was despondent from time to time. At least one would think so. Or was he only undecided? In either case, Jeanne d'Arc constantly encouraged him. The words of the Bastard of Orléans affirm this: 'She urged the king very urgently, and very often with the message to hurry and no longer to procrastinate.'[15]

The cardinal capacity of leaders may be their ability to decide on the specific form of behaviour that is applicable and appropriate in the present situation. This ability is possibly a universal aspect of effective leadership. But in this case, I would rather talk about 'good judgement'.[16] The primary characteristic of Jeanne La Pucelle was not that she was fresh, convincing, confident, energetic or brave, but that she was blessed with 'good judgement'.[17] Precisely this core competency was continually confirmed in a series of victories, a necessary luxury, for 'no leader, however great, can long continue unless he wins victories'.[18]

Here is an interesting quote from Field Marshall Montgomery that relates to the above:

'The acid test of an officer who aspires to high command is his ability to be able to grasp quickly the essentials of a military problem, to decide swiftly what he will do, to make it clear to all concerned what he intends to achieve and how he will do it, and then to see that his subordinate commanders get on with the job. Above all, he has to...concentrate on the essentials, and on those details and only those details which are necessary to the proper carrying out of his plan – trusting his staff to effect all the necessary co-ordination. When all is said and done the greatest quality required in a commander is "decision"; he must then be able to issue clear orders and have the "drive" to get things done.'[19]

A characteristic feature of Jeanne's leadership is that, as mentioned, she almost always led from the front. In every attack she commanded, she always went in first. Her fellow fighters repeatedly confirmed this.[20] Jeanne thus brought camaraderie, trust and unity among the soldiers, made 'war' into teamwork, and reached out to everyone with her unyielding will to win. Everyone saw her on the battlefield, and everyone saw her brimming self-confidence, the total lack of fear and the demonstration of her indomitable will, both in her actions and in her words and gestures. It was as if it was the most natural thing in the world, to be so determined and controlled amidst noise, dust, the clatter of weapons, the screams of the wounded and the ever-present 'friction'. Yet something equally important needs to be mentioned: Jeanne wanted her soldiers to *confess* before the battle, thus – as a true leader – she prepared her fighters for death, or at least for serious injuries.[21]

As for her 'leading from the front', the similarity between Jeanne and Rommel is striking. Rommel, like our heroine, was a typical 'front line commander'.[22] 'During [his actions at Dinant] he worked like a devil, popping up where the fights were the most violent, screaming commands and personally offering a helping hand where necessary.' On 12 June 1940 he personally led the attack on Saint Valéry (northern France) in which 46000 French were captured.[23] In short, there existed between Rommel and his troops that mutual understanding that cannot be explained or analysed but – according to one of his subordinates – 'must be considered a gift from the gods'.[24]

Rommel, incidentally, acted entirely in accordance with the general German tactics on the battlefield in the Second World War. General Manstein even believes that this modus operandi has traditionally been the 'forte' of German military leadership, since it expects its commanders to show initiative, seize opportunities, be prepared to accept responsibility and generally do everything that favours these qualities.[25]

Q. Was Jeanne an effective commander or was she something more than that?

A. According to Sun Tzu, the Chinese general in the 4th-3rd century BCE, a good and effective commander must have a certain psychological profile. He should be 'generous', 'bold but not reckless', and 'steadfast without being stubborn'. In dignity, knowledge, and courage, he must be superior to his subordinates. In maintaining the discipline, he will be righteous. And if necessary, he will even amend orders received from higher powers if unforeseen circumstances dictate this,[26] provided that situational corrections do not conflict with three immutable strategic principles which, according to the Chinese general, should be respected in all circumstances. These 'fundamental invariants'[27], are: (1) the 'freedom of action' in time and space (so that one does not play into the enemy's hands – which is the case if the latter is the strategic attacker), (2) the prescribed 'proportionality between purpose and means',[28] (3) 'the maintenance of the unit of one's own resources against the division of the enemy's resources' (troops are divided when they cannot give each other mutual support).[29]

Striking in this sketch of Sun Tzu's teachings is that the word 'trust' is not mentioned at all, a word that dominates in Western commentary. In the West it is the most essential criterion, which I will now consider.

'Winning the men's trust,' writes Rommel, 'sets high demands on a commander. He must proceed with caution, take care of his men, just live as they do and – above all – practice self-discipline. But once he has gained their confidence, his men will follow him through thick and thin.'[30] General Grant, commander of the Confederates in the American Civil War, is known to have created boundless trust in his soldiers; he, conversely, had the same confidence in his men.[31]

The fact is that the soldiers followed the Maid. Their trust was limitless. These are the words of Jean de Metz: 'I had absolute faith in her. Her words and her ardent faith in God inflamed me. I believe she was sent from God.'[32] Here follows an impression of Jeanne's appearance and behaviour that invoked that faith. It is a simple but intensely suggestive account by Georges Chastellain [historian of Philip the Good and absolutely no friend of Jeanne's[33]]. He was inspired to write this account when he observed Jeanne when she sallied out of Compiègne, having her date with destiny:

'She mounted her horse, armed as would be a man, adorned in a doublet of rich cloth of gold over her armor. She rode a gray steed, very handsome and very proud, and displayed herself in the armor and manners that a captain who leads a large army would. And in that state, with her standard raised high and blowing in the wind, and accompanied by many noble men, around four hours before midday, she charged out of town.'[34]

Of course, many others have also characterised a good commander. For instance, Napoleon said that the best general was he who makes the fewest mistakes (or who causes the fewest mistakes, as we would say today because of the increased distance between general and battlefield).[35]

Liddell Hart also summed up a series of characteristics. He ranked among them 'creative intelligence' and a 'powerful personality' (closely linked to determination).[36] And Field Marshal Montgomery wrote: 'To exercise high command in a war successfully, a commander in chief has to have an inner conviction, which, at times, will transcend reason. Having fought, possibly over a prolonged period, for the advantage and gained it, there then comes the moment for boldness. When that moment comes, will he throw his bonnet over the mill and soar from the known to seize the unknown? In the answer to that question lies the supreme test of generalship in high command.'[37]

Acknowledging all that has just been said, I contend that Jeanne did not only instil boundless trust but in addition boosted the morale of her warriors.[38] For although even the bravest man in her army had known moments when fear dictated his actions, those moments of weakness evaporated when Jeanne stormed forward with her standard.

The importance of 'morale' as a state of consciousness cannot be stressed enough. It is that intangible, spiritual power that can make a whole group of people go beyond their limits. Of course, the commander must at least have that 'unbending willpower' and 'an unwavering self-confidence'.[39] But for the capture of Les Tourelles, even willpower and self-confidence were not enough, as we will see below.

Whichever way one interprets the Maid, even her critics do not have the slightest doubt about Jeanne's ability to instil confidence as well as her perseverance, steadiness, creative intelligence, generosity, grandeur, knowledge, courage and virtue.

---

1. Mongomery, cited in Connelly (2002), p.151.
2. Quoted by Holden (1991), p.4 of 14 of a downloaded file.
3. Quoted in Pernoud (1962), p.133.
4. Sibley & Frey (2008), p.88.
5. Pernoud & Clin (2011), p.153. The chief judge was Bishop Cauchon, then chief negotiator at the conclusion of the Treaty of Troyes.
6. Cf. Richey (2000), p.16 van 32 of a downloaded file.
7. But she always chose her words very carefully.
8. Virion (1972), p.178.
9. This belief is especially prevalent in 'firms in dynamic environments where it is more important to have major product innovations', Yukl, p.246.
10. Hobbins (2012), p.231.
11. DeVries (2011), p.46.
12. DeVries (2011), p.70.
13. See Yukl (1998), p.76.
14. Williams (2005), p.107 on Maréchal Pétain who knew such moments.

15. Pernoud (1962), p.127. Freely translated.
16. According to Yukl (1998, 57), researchers should not only be satisfied with behavioural classifications (task or relationship oriented) but also concern themselves with the more 'specific functional content of this behavior'.
17. 'Decision analysis' is therefore crucial in the study of leadership. Regarding the question of what exactly 'good judgement' entails, a whole discipline is devoted to the matter under the name of 'decision theory'.
18. Cf. Montgomery, quoted in Connelly (2002), p.151.
19. Quoted in Connelly (2002), p.156
20. Richey (2000), p.4 van 32 of a downloaded file.
21. Cf. Harold G. Moore in Connelly (2002), p.214/15.
22. Rommel's habit of commanding from the frontlines almost cost him his life several times. This habit provoked criticism – even from his own staff. It happened that Rommel, at a crucial moment, could not be reached at headquarters for two days. Similar things occurred during the attack on Tobroek. Rommel's personal involvement in small battles sometimes led to serious mistakes. On the other hand, he could assess a confused situation himself.
23. Sibley and Fry (2008), p.76/77. And then there is his behavior during the English offensive [Operation Crusader] in North Africa: 'In contrast to the commanders of his opponents, Rommel was [like Jeanne] in the front lines, and at a certain point, he personally took command of a pair of 88-mm guns.' Ibid. p.112.
24. Quoted in Connelly (2002), p.101.
25. Manstein, quoted in Connelly (2002), p.146.
26. See De Vos (2006), p.33/34.
27. Newman (1942), p.12.
28. Spreading misleading information can increase the freedom of action. The same goes for moving the government to a safer place. Mantel (1931), p.133.
29. De Vos (2006), p.33/34. See also Wing (1988).
30. See Sibley & Fry (2008), p.22.
31. Connelly (2002), p.51.
32. Rehabilitation, 04, p.2 of 5 of a downloaded file.
33. Chastellain used to call Jeanne 'that woman' ('ceste femme'). Thomas (2000), p.475.
34. Fabre (1948, Dutch translation), p.222. See also Pernoud & Clin (2011), p.139.
35. Liddell Hart (1944), p.221.
36. Liddell Hart (1944), p.222/23.
37. Montgomery (1961), p.52.
38. Mantel (1931), p.128.
39. Ibid.

20 JEANNE AS A CHARISMATIC COMMANDER

'There is a soul to an army as well as to the individual man, and no general can accomplish the full work of his army unless he commands the soul of his men, as well as their bodies and legs.'[1]
- General Sherman

In the days of La Pucelle there was no 'chain of command'. Whether decisions were taken at the court, or on the spot in a tent in the field, commanders seem to have made decisions through ad hoc committees of leaders in which the most powerful speaker could triumph. And it was indeed the Maid, who, young as she was, imposed her will many times in the meetings of hardened, mature men in the prime of their life. This exceptional circumstance is beyond any doubt. 'The cumulative testimony of her comrades-in-arms,' writes Richey (2000), 'shows that Jeanne was no mere inspirational figurehead. She was repeatedly present when key decisions were being made in councils of war and she repeatedly forced those decisions to reflect her expressed will.'[2] 'Jeanne,' he continues, 'was the ultimate driving power behind every aggressive move the French army made.'[3]

The French saint was no ordinary 'excellent' leader or commander. She was much more, she was a *charismatic* commander. Her hero status alone attracted many fighters, mobilised the army and stimulated the soldiers, especially when they could actually see and hear her.

The latter, for example, was the reason the army commanders chose to involve Jeanne in the attack on Paris on 8 September 1429, exactly the day – the birth of Virgin Mary – on which she had not wanted to attack. The army commanders deceived her by telling her that it was in fact a preparatory exercise and that she did not have to take it to heart. During her trial, Jeanne talked about it as follows: It was at the request of 'des nobles gens d'armes' who wanted an 'escarmouche.' But she added that she – once in action – planned to 'move further and cross the canals of Paris,' not by order of her voices 'but also not in breach of their advice.'[4]

* * *

Q. How could it be that Jeanne's followers, including army commanders, were willing to share the Maid's firm conviction, eventually accepting her completely, being affectionate to her, trusting her blindly, and in addition – at the risk of death or mutilation – were willing to fight for her as lions?

This question brings us to the very heart of her charismatic leadership. For only charismatic leadership explains the excessive amount of confidence ('morale') that must have been present at the capture of Les Tourelles.

What is charisma? Is it a divine gift, such as performing miracles or predicting the future? Or is it, as Max Weber claims, a form of influence that is not based on tradition or formal authority but on the perception of the followers that their hero is endowed with extraordinary qualities?[5] Possibly, but is the latter explanation not too one-sided? Is charisma rather the result of the attributes of the leader ('nature'), *in conjunction with* 'nourishing' environmental conditions (in the case of the Maid: the enemy, *timing*, stress levels and perceptions of her followers[6])? In circles of postmodern authors there is a leaning towards seeing the environment as a dominant influence.[7] That is certainly exaggerated, because 'nurture' implies 'nature' and vice versa. After all, a phenomenon can only happen if the potential for it is there from the outset. And if potential is not provoked and nourished, then there is no possibility for a talent to emerge.

Anyway, necessary elements for charisma are (a) moral qualities, (b) an absolutely exceptional willpower and (c) astonishing self-confidence. These three key features were unified in Jeanne La Pucelle. But did it stop here?

At this point in the book, the reader is adequately informed about the willpower and self-confidence of Jeanne d'Arc, and equally so about her heroic behaviour in the moral sense. What we now have to underline is the additional dimension of *religion*. It is indisputable that Jeanne believed in the divine origins of her mission. This belief was even the fundament of her mission, a mission that, through its successes, positively fed back into her willpower, self-confidence and the morale of her troops. Her touching sense of truth, sacrifice, sincerity, optimism, and regard for the Eucharist (she tried to get everyone to go to Holy Mass) are well documented. This led to an enhancement of the motivating force, another effect of charismatic leadership.[8] Her performance in battles was pure to the highest degree. She forbade all forms of looting, something that was unheard of in those days (looting was a means to finance war[9]). More generally, the blessed Maid brought discipline into the army because it learned to respect God and the Holy Mass. And her virtuous life delighted the general public.

All the facts about Jeanne d'Arc, whichever way you look at them, speak of the fact that the religious factor played a decisive role. In the eyes of the people and the French nobility, Jeanne was holy from the outset. And as a result, her word was sure, convincing, true and inspiring.

Moreover, the mysticism surrounding the coronation gave rise to strong emotions, emotions that were comparable to the enthusiasm to go crusading – something that only happens when people are convinced that God is on their side. It was these overwhelming, religious emotions that brought knights and ordinary fighters to the triumphant caravan of Jeanne La Pucelle. The latter *embodied* in a unique way the religious patriotism of a group, an 'incarnation' which was emphasised by religious banners, crosses, processions and so on. **The sanctity of a miraculous creature in combination with the mysticism surrounding the coronation was thus at the heart of the matter.**

This was by no means coincidental. In moments of great misery or great joy, the masses have a natural tendency to turn to something 'superhuman' to discover the symbol of their need for admiration or protection. When de Gaulle was present on the historic 'Liberation Walk' on the Champs Élysées in 1944, no one cried out 'vive la France!' but everywhere people shouted 'vive de Gaulle'.[10] And de Gaulle was not a saint![11]

A chivalrous element also played a part. That Jeanne d'Arc was a female warrior was a cardinal part of her charisma. This is also inextricably linked to religion. The army is and remains – especially in the subculture of the more elitist levels – a male affair in which women are only admitted if they perform as well as men *and do not lose their femininity*. This is feasible for very few women. But when a young woman demonstrates the strength and courage that makes her the equal of men, her feminine charm is rather an advantage than a disadvantage.[12] Such a woman wins the 'hearts and minds' of men.

Various testimonies indicate that Jeanne possessed exactly such irresistible charm: she was young, attractive, powerful, brave, and did not complain about hardships; she was playful, cried easily and showed compassion for all wounded and dying warriors, friend and foe alike. After the Battle of Patay, she held the head of a dying English soldier in her lap to comfort him as he died. Stephen Richey says it very eloquently in his splendid essay: 'She was strong and fierce when her men wanted a warrior comrade who was strong and fierce. She was gentle and kind when they most needed to be near a woman who was gentle and kind.'[13] In short, the men did not only sense a holy goodness in her, but also experienced a transcendental, exalted, sublimated devotional love for her,[14] *a courtly love that is only possible in a religious culture*. This is the reason why Jeanne d'Arc is incomprehensible outside a medieval, Catholic context. The chivalrous element cannot be detached from the context of a pious, Catholic culture.

The secret of the saint of Orléans was that she had the power to make thousands of armed men fall in love with her, not romantically, but as 'the living focus of their hunger to serve a higher cause'.[15] *'Whenever Jeanne rose in her stirrups to shout "Let all who love me – follow me!" over all the din, she was exploiting a special relationship between leader and led that is unique in all history.'*[16] *'Ultimately, it was this astonishing ability of Joan's to make an army of soldiers chastely love her [to the point that they would willingly face death in battle for her] that empowered her to bodily shove history into a new path.'*[17] *An androgynous person would never have been able to evoke these feelings, at least not in real men. These men perceived her as an angel sent from God. Or at least as a blessed virgin.*

---

1. Quoted in Connelly (2002), p.24.
2. Richey (2000), p.13 of 32 of a downloaded file.
3. Ibid.
4. Quoted in Pernoud (1962), p.158. See also Hobbins (2012), p.121 juncto p.130.
5. According to Max Weber, a charismatic leader has a strong sense of 'vocation' and looks more like a quasi-religious 'hero' (that is, someone who stands outside the everyday world), than a normal, democratic politician. Rees (2013), p.12, 116.
6. Charismatic leadership is in any case more likely in stressful and transitional situations, especially if formal authority has failed and traditional values and beliefs are disputed. As to whether 'social turmoil' as such is also necessary, opinions differ. Only the psychoanalytical theory explicitly requires a social (or personal) crisis. See Yukl (1998).
7. See Yukl (1998), paragraph 12.
8. See Yukl (1998), p.244.
9. Tuchman (1982), p.105.
10. According to George Bidault. See Williams (2005).
11. At the summit in Yalta, Roosevelt told Stalin that de Gaulle had compared himself to Jeanne d'Arc. Whether this is really true is not certain, especially since Roosevelt had a personal dislike of de Gaulle. Gardner (1964), p.56.
12. Cf. Richey (2000), p.18 of 32 of a downloaded file.

13. Richey (2000), p.19 of 32 of a downloaded file.
14. Cf. Richey (2000), p.19 of 32 of a downloaded file.
15. Richey (2000), p.19 of 32 of a downloaded file. Roughly translated.
16. Richey (2000), p.19/20 of 32 of a downloaded file.
17. Ibid.

21 THE SIGNIFICANCE OF PERSONALITY IN WAR AND POLITICS

'Alexander, not Macedonia conquered the world.
Scipio, not Rome destroyed Carthage.
Marlborough, not the allies defeated France.'
- General Patton

War and politics involve (a) balancing 'power vectors' and (b) accommodating political personalities like Hitler, Mussolini, Mao, Churchill and Roosevelt. None of these leaders acted in a vacuum. They were influenced by (a) lobbies of private stakeholders (such as media conglomerates, arms factories, NGOs, oil companies) and (b) government bureaucracy determining the available options for a president or prime minister.[1]

Both private organisations and state departments act through individuals, that is to say: through 'embodied intelligences' that act according to various concepts of national, organisational and personal importance. These people, however, do not decide in a rational way (although one can make it look so in retrospect). In reality, managers and politicians decide by 'wheeling and dealing' regardless of how and where. In such a climate 'personality' plays a weighty role. *The 'hard core' of governmental politics is therefore personality.*²

All actions by the aforementioned actors are therefore in principle unpredictable, because the boss is (also) only participating in this 'wheeling and dealing' between personalities who are all endowed with 'bargaining advantages' and persuasive force. Governmental governance, seen in this light, exists in the game of 'bargaining' between relatively independent players. It is a game that takes place in certain, regulated – rarely public – communication channels. Influencing factors, in addition to personal peculiarities, are therefore (a) the choice of the channel, and (b) the journey through the channel.³

In so far as typical group decisions occur, the unpredictable mechanisms of 'group decision-making' are in play. Politics, especially at the international level, is – because of all this – a conglomerate of emotion, ambition, greed, and revenge ('tit for tat'). This statement applies to all times, including the 'waning of the Middle Ages' – the time of Jeanne d'Arc – no matter how embryonic these tendencies were then. For example, you will discover this conglomerate in the struggle between Philip the Good and the Dauphin [which was incorporated into the Hundred Years' War], or in the battle between 'the camarilla of Trémoïlle' and Jeanne d'Arc. At its core, 'politics' is characterised by the fact that – just as in love – in exercising power 'no rivals' are tolerated. Every management but also every interpretation of (international) politics is, given the truth of this basic statement, and all that it implies, exceedingly uncertain, even when it is assumed that history is guided. Jeanne's deepest vocation was opposing human squabbling with 'La Royauté de notre Seigneur Jésus-Christ'.

Jeanne was able to accomplish her political and religious mission only because she was blessed with a magnetic, religious personality, that is to say with imagination, willpower, a burning faith, persuasion, and specific abilities 'to make an army of soldiers chastely love her – to the point that they would willingly face death in battle for her.'[4]

---

1. With regard to the options offered by bureaucracy, Kennedy's (rational) 'measured response' in international conflicts with military aspects is an interesting case. In their book *Essence of Decision*, Allison & Zelikow (1999) demonstrate how his options and decisions were partly determined by the advisory organisations that Kennedy's administration consulted. Allison & Zelikow (1999).
2. Allison & Zelikow (1999), p.297.
3. Allison & Zelikow (1999).
4. Richey (2000), p.21 of 32 of a downloaded file.

EPILOGUE

'Jeanne was a being so uplifted from the ordinary run of mankind that she finds no equal in a thousand years'
- Churchill

The saying 'that famous figures eventually become legendary' does not apply to Jeanne. The facts of her life were *already* legendary. The breaking of the siege of Orléans, for instance, *immediately* amazed the world. 'What happened then,' declared d'Alençon during the rehabilitation process, 'is simply a miracle, something that lies outside the power of the people.' This was also the opinion of the army commanders and the soldiers.[1] In a few days the French saint did not only triumph militarily, but also completely reversed the established moral order on the battlefields of the Hundred Years' War; she made sure that an army of 'habitual losers' started to see itself in a new light.[2]

The post-modern, anti-religious world has tried to devalue these facts, so to distort the epic of Jeanne d'Arc, to take the saint out of her Catholic medieval context and remove all supernatural elements. But such a *deconstruction* is totally pointless. It is indeed like a review of Ayrolles' monumental work on Jeanne claims: only faithful Catholics can have the final say on this life and this mission – the virtues, the deeds, the success, the martyrdom, and the fame of the Maid.[3]

Only faithful Catholics can understand and repeat that the heavenly Maid in the words of Virion (1972) – was not merely a 'libératrice', a martyr of the nation as well as the inspired catalyst 'du beau mystère de Reims', but also the messenger of (a) the eternal principles of politics, (b) the unchanging principles of natural administrative power, and (c) the conditions for true peace. For faithful Catholics, saint Jeanne d'Arc is therefore nothing less than the envoy of a heavenly wisdom.[4]

Taylor (2010), in her book *The Virgin Warrior*, does not understand this religious vision. She thinks that if the life of Jeanne La Pucelle had been God's work, the pure girl would have suffered nothing. And it gets even more confusing. While the French saint continually relied on God's intervention, Taylor distorts this fact into the claim that Jeanne had full confidence in her own capacities. However, in order to claim the latter, one must inevitably *rewrite* history. Jeanne herself, notwithstanding her unwavering self-confidence, explicitly trusted in God and nothing else. Of course, much can be said about the unique character of Jeanne d'Arc. But now that the reader has arrived at this epilogue, he or she has read all I had to say about this matter.

We have seen how an illiterate, immaculate 17-year-old peasant girl without military experience became commander in the king's army because there was no rational, orthodox alternative; everything had been tried and everything had failed. We have seen how everyone was amazed by the girl and her knowledge, especially her plan to break the will of the English through the mystery surrounding the coronation, a daring feat of military and political thinking.

We have also learned the secret of Jeanne: the power to make thousands of armed men chastely fall in love with her, as 'the living focus of their hunger to serve a higher, religious purpose'. And we have concluded that it was this amazing power that made the pure and brave girl, in conjunction with her martyrdom, famous.

We have seen how only **a shining strategic goal** creates leadership that fosters commitment, and not merely compliancy. In the present case, it was a matter of the right of every nation to have a territory on which no wars of aggression may be carried out, thus *the right to defend the soul of your own nation*. It was precisely because of this that Jeanne wanted to bring about a unique moral, psychological and emotional mobilisation of the French nation. The special thing about her was that she not only linked this patriotism to informed strategic thinking, but that she mingled it...with religion.[5]

No one can deny that religion played a central role in Jeanne's prestigious mission, if only because she went to Holy Mass as often as possible and urged others to do the same. Perhaps Montgomery thought of something similar when he wrote that he did not believe that a commander could inspire an army or even an individual without any understanding of something like a 'religious truth'.[6] 'And yet,' writes Stephen Richey (2000) – echoing Johan Huizinga,[7] Churchill,[8] and Barbara Tuchman[9] – 'every analysis of saint Jeanne d'Arc must end with the finding that that there is something about her that will be forever beyond our grasp.' Well said, Richey, because there is indeed something fundamentally mysterious to her, something 'otherworldly', something 'godlike' as Dunois expressed it.

After all, 'who – God aside – would have been able to move the Crown Council and the commanders to follow the view of a young girl at the risk – in case of failure – to be doused with libel as never before occurred in history?' [Jean Gerson.] Who could have imagined the journey from Blois turning into a religious procession, with priests bearing the cross and singing hymns? Moreover, did not Jeanne herself say during her trial 'that she came from God?'[10] In fact, she even asked 'to be returned to God, where she came from',[11] a request that is entirely in line with her statement that when her voices said goodbye to her, she used to cry because she had fain been picked up by them and carried to those superior realms. Everything about Jeanne d'Arc was divinely inspired, especially her political and military intuition. Without that heavenly inspiration, Jeanne La Pucelle was and remains an infinitely deep mystery.

---

1. Rehabilitation, 07.
2. Richey (2000), p.7 of 32 of a downloaded file.
3. Quoted in Thomas (2000), p.585.
4. Virion (1972), p.232/33.
5. Slim, quoted in Connelly (2002), p.163.
6. Quoted in Connelly (2002), p.154.
7. 'We are seeking in vain for the term that resumes Jeanne d'Arc's being... Heroine does not meet. Genius even less. Saint, even if one cannot understand it perfectly in the technical ecclesiastical sense, meets this term by far the best.' Quoted in Heering (1948).
8. See the quotation in Chapter 26.
9. Barbara Tuchman: 'The Jeanne d'Arc phenomenon surpasses all understanding.' Tuchman (1982), p.655.
10. More complete and untranslated: 'qu'elle vint de par Dieu, et qu'elle n'a que faire ici.' Procès de condamnation, séance du 24 Février. http://www.stejeannedarc.net/condamnation/interro_public3.php, accessed 13 May 2015.
11. Full quote: 'Je demande qu'on me renvoie à Dieu d'où je suis venue.' Quoted in Pernoud & Clin (2011), p.253.

APPENDIX I

THE POLITICAL CONTEXT

France in the days of Jeanne d'Arc was a multitude of duchies and counties that formed provinces. At the head of these 'pays' and 'patria' were the twelve 'pairs' of France. These paladins competed among themselves on various rights, a situation that was a direct consequence of the feudal order that ensured the vertical relations between lord and vassal, but regulated nothing in the horizontal relationships between each other's peers. As a result, medieval France was divided and the inhabitants formed as many small, hostile 'nations'.[1]

At the same time, there was a power struggle between the kings striving for centralisation[2] and dukes and earls striving for independence. [The ambition of the latter, of course, contrasted with their promised faithfulness to the dynasty.][3] In such a situation of deconcentration and fragmentation, only an anointed monarch could still bind together the different 'provinces'. Only sacral kingship could provide sufficient authority to curb the centrifugal forces in such an unstable context.[4]

The internal struggle for dominion over parts of France was complicated by the interference of the English royal house. The latter claimed France on the basis of the Treaty of Troyes. The French, on the other hand, adhered to the ancient Franconian law that recognises only succession in the male line. Only Burgundy could have an English king for the reasons outlined below.

Almost two decades before the Treaty of Troyes, the Duke of Orléans (Louis) and the Duke of Burgundy (John the Fearless) were eager to play a leading role in France, particularly in Paris. After the murder of Louis of Orléans (1407) by John the Fearless (which he attempted to justify as a tyrannicide) the rivalry between Louis and John led to the emergence of two factions. One faction, the party of the Armagnacs, supported the Dauphinist Frenchmen; the other, the faction of the Bourguignons, backed Burgundy. The battle between these factions was accompanied by a smear campaign in which the Dauphin was characterised as a bastard of the adulterous queen (Isabella of Bavaria).

In 1419, John the Fearless – possibly with the knowledge of the Dauphin – was beaten to death with an axe as a reprisal for the murder of Louis of Orléans. This murder created great unrest in Paris and led to the Treaty of Troyes (1420) between Philip the Good (the son of John the Fearless) and the English King (Henry V). Philip the Good was determined to avenge his father and wanted to assure himself of English support. This pact is one of the greatest humiliations France has suffered and comparable to the surrender to the Germans in 1940. The treaty claimed the French throne for Henry V and disinherited the Dauphin because of his alleged share in the murder of John the Fearless. As a result of all this dynastic disruption, a civil war erupted that became part of the Hundred Years' War (see Appendix II).

It was in this context that the mentally ill Charles VI, the father of Charles VII, ruled France. His condition created a vacuum that was filled by his regent and wife Isabella of Bavaria, a woman who was more English than French minded.[5]

On 22 October 1422 'Charles le Fou' died. Coincidentally, just a few months earlier, Henry V of England had also passed away. Now the situation foreseen in the Treaty of Troyes became reality. According to the treaty, with the death of Charles VI, the rule of the underage Henry VI began (with Bedford as regent). Henry VI's accession to the throne coincided with the reign of Charles VI. The same day, the Dauphin – at the age of 19 – was dubbed king of France by his circle. One of the two pretenders had to be removed.

The whole of the North and the East – some enclaves (including Vaucouleurs and Orléans) aside – were occupied by the English invading army, which had been led by Henry V. [The goal of Henry V was to conquer France province by province[6] and eventually be crowned king of England and France.] Only the Dauphin, 'le roi de Bourges', represented France. In the time of Jeanne d'Arc, therefore, France was plagued by various military campaigns,[7] as well as looting. No one in France was sure of his life and possessions; anyone could be kidnapped only to be released against a ransom;[8] even whole castles were conquered by itinerant robbers; travelling was very dangerous and every village and town could be faced with paying protection money under the threat of arbitrary executions and arson.[9]

---

1. These clusters were in turn divided into a multitude of domains and fiefs whose owners lived in a constant state of war. In addition to this division and multiplicity at the provincial level, there was a 'sustained rivalry

between cities and villages, even of villages among themselves; and from one valley to another.' Evans (1959), p.38/39.
2. Including the associated institutionalisation.
3. This faithlessness was one of the causes of the collapse of the feudal system, and thus of the administrative order; for countries and (real) nations did not exist yet so that the whole order depended on the faithfulness that the vassal swore to his king. Another cause was the emergence of *cities* where the guilds produced – against money – firearms and gunpowder which undermined the power of the nobility.
4. Slowly but surely the kings of France reduced the power of the vassals and established their sovereignty over France. See Evans (1959) for the role of the Crusades in this process.
5. Isabella of Bavaria would later be regarded as the evil genius behind France's misery, possibly as a result of a slander campaign by the English. The common people sympathised with the sick Charles VI, perhaps also as the result of a propaganda campaign. Processions to pray for the king and letter campaigns detailing John the Fearless' dealings with the English formed part of the latter.
6. His campaign started in Normandy. Incidentally, the fundamental objective of Philip the Good, after the death of Jeanne d'Arc, seems to have been the purification of the Ile de France through a decentralised war (with attacks in the Hinterland of the enemy). See Thomas (2000), p.443.
7. And by plundering English deserters (including those from Gascony, which was then an English fiefdom).
8. A ransom could consist of money, horses, wine or weapons.
9. The whole of England was flooded with the proceeds from the looting of France. See Seward (2003), p.81.

APPENDIX II

THE MILITARY SITUATION

Jeanne was aware of the general military situation, at least according to Jean de Metz.[1] But how? Through her father and her own experience of passing looters? Or through the stories exchanged between villagers? The facts, which Jeanne must have known (or suspected), are the following:

Edward III, since 1134 the enemy of Valois King Philip VI, invades France. The basis for this incursion is the confiscation by Philip of the Duchy of Guyenne ('Gascony') which was on loan but still partly English.

Battle of Crécy (1346). More than 10000 French soldiers are massacred by English archers.[2]

Battle of Poitiers (1356): The Black Prince, son of Edward III, defeats the Valois King Jean le Bon (circa 2500 French soldiers perish, including many knights; almost as many were captured, including Jean le Bon himself).

Battle of Agincourt (1415): Henry V defeats the 20 000

man army of the Dauphin with 10 000 men;[3] The French were devastated as the nobility associated with the traditional centre was decimated. [5000 French nobles perished.]

1418. **The English enter Paris**, thanks to the Duke of Burgundy (John the Fearless).

Battle of Cravant (1423). Bedford and Salisbury (one of Bedford's army commanders) defeat the French; almost 1200 French (and even more Scottish) soldiers succumb. The Champagne region is now largely governed by England.

Verneuil (1424): This is a second Agincourt in which the French suffer a devastating loss.

1427. **Bedford** attacks – as part of a large summer offensive[4] – Montargis. He is defeated by the French, headed by the Bastard of Orléans and Étienne de Vignolles ('La Hire').

Bedford continues his offensive; his troops occupy Laval.

On 22 June 1428, **Bedford** announces that only Vaucouleurs has still to be conquered. Although Bedford is against the siege of Orléans, it is decided ('God knoweth by what advis,' Bedford)[5] to take Orléans. The city is defended by the Bastard of Orléans.

Orléans is encircled on 17 October 1428, albeit not completely.[6] Both the English and the French send supplies, to the siege army and the trapped residents of Orléans, respectively. In order to get at the English goods, the French attack the supply convoy. This results in the Battle of the Herring (at Rouvray), another French defeat.[7]

---

1. Taylor (2010), p.37.
2. These archers used longbows.

3. The Dauphin's army was headed by the Dukes of Orléans, Bourbon, Alençon and Bretagne. The Dauphin himself was not there.
4. With Mont Saint Michel and Vaucouleurs as vertices.
5. Bedford, summer 1429, in a letter to Henry VI.
6. It is during this operation that Thomas Montagu, Earl of Salisbury, dies after being struck in the face by a cannonball; John Talbot becomes his successor.
7. Several high-ranking Frenchmen (Clermont, Regnault de Chartres, La Hire and others) plus 2000 soldiers from Clermont, left Orléans, unhindered by the English. The Bastard of Orléans also went along but only to persuade the fleeing soldiers to return; a few days later the Bastard returned to Orléans.

PRINCIPAL CHARACTERS

Alençon (Jean II of = d'Alençon): A general in the army of the king in the last phase of the Hundred Years' War, commander-in-chief of the Loire offensive. He was Jeanne's most loyal ally.

Bastard of Orléans: Jean d'Orléans, the later Count of Dunois, was the illegitimate son of Louis I, Duke of Orléans and his mistress Mariette d'Enghien.

Braudicourt (Robert de): Castellan and captain of the royal garrison at Vaucouleurs.

Charles VII: King of France from 1422 to his death in 1461. Almost immediately after his accession to the title of Dauphin, Charles had to face threats to his inheritance and was forced to flee from Paris on 29 May 1418.

Clausewitz (Carl von): A Prussian general and military theorist.

Duke of Burgundy: see Philip the Good.

Dunois: see Bastard of Orléans.

Fastolf: English career soldier who fought in the second phase of the Hundred Years' War. His name is immortalised through William Shakespeare's character 'Falstaff'.

Henry V: The second English monarch of the House of Lancaster, known and celebrated as one of the greatest warrior kings of medieval England.

La Hire (= Etienne de Vignolles): Although not a noble, La Hire was a very capable military leader. He was a close comrade of Jeanne d'Arc and one of the few military leaders who *really* believed in her.

Liddell Hart: A British soldier, military historian and military theorist who recommended the 'indirect approach'. Among other books, he was the author of The History of World War II.

Montgomery: A senior British Army officer (field marshal) who fought in both the First World War and the Second World War.

Philip the Good (= Duke of Burgundy): A member of the Valois dynasty to which all the 15th century kings of France belonged. He alternated between alliances with the English and the French in an attempt to improve his dynasty's position.

Regnault de Chartres: Duke and archbishop of Reims; also grand chancellor of France. He participated in the Orléans war council.

Richmont (Arthur de): A leading military commander who briefly sided with the English, but otherwise remained firmly committed to Charles VII. He was appointed Constable of

France and played an important role in assuring the final defeat of the English in the Hundred Years' War.

Rommel: German Field Marshal who gained the respect of his enemies as commander of the Afrika Korps in the Second World War.

Tremoïlle (George, de la): A powerful advisor who exercised considerable influence over Charles VII. At first allied with Philip the Good in the power struggle during Charles VI's madness, Trémoille switched his loyalty when the rival faction, the Armagnacs, came into power.

Xaintrailles (Jean Poton de): A minor noble and one of Jeanne's chief lieutenants.

BIBLIOGRAPHY

Allison, G. & P. Zelikow. 1999.

Essence of Decision. New York: Longman.

Ammers-Küller, Van, J. 1952.

De Koning en de heks. Amsterdam: Engelhard, van Embden & Co.

Battistelli, P.P. 2011.

Heinz Guderian. Oxford: Osprey Publishing.

Baylis, J. et al. 1975.

Contemporary Strategy. London: Croom Helm.

Beaudry, I. 2000.

The military Genius of Jeanne d'Arc, and the Concept of Victory.

https://archive.schillerinstitute.com/educ/joan_ib.html. Accessed 28 February 2020.

Beaufre, A. 1965.

Introduction to Strategy. London: Faber and Faber.

Barnaby, F. (ed.). 1984.

Future War. London: Michael Joseph.

Clausewitz, Von, C. 1987.

On War. Harmondsworth: Penguin books.

Connelly, O. 2002.

On War and Leadership. Princeton: Princeton University Press.

Creveld, Van, M. 2001.

Men, Women & War. London: Cassell & Co.

Creveld, Van, M. 2007.

De evolutie van de oorlog. Utrecht: Spectrum.

Creveld, Van, M. 2008.

The Culture of War. New York: Ballantine Books.

Critchley, J. 1978.

Feudalism. London: George Allen & Unwin.

De Vos, L. 2006.

Strategie & tactiek. Leuven: Davidsfonds.

DeVries, K. 2011,

Joan of Arc. A military Leader. Gloucestershire: The History Press.

Bont, D. et al. (red.). 1943.

De katholieke Kerk. Godsdienstleer en apologie. Utrecht:

Het Spectrum. Part II, book 19: Deugdenleer ('virtue ethics').

Earle E.M. et al.(eds). 1960.

Makers of modern Strategy. Princeton: Princeton University Press.

Engelstad, C.F. 1988.

In het land der levenden. (A book about Gilles De Rais, the child serial killer who fought alongside Joan Of Arc). Schoorl: Conserve.

Evans, J. 1959.

Leven in de Middeleeuwen.

Antwerp: De Haan/Standaard.

Fabre, L. 1948.

Joan of Arc. English version 1954. London: Odhams Press.

Fabre, L. 1948.

De Maagd van Orleans. Dutch version 1955.

Utrecht: Het Spectrum.

Forty, G. & A. Forty. 1997.

Women War Heroines. London: Arms and Armour Press.

Gardner, B. 1964.

Het verspeelde uur. Baarn: Het Wereldvenster.

Gordon, M. 2001.

Jeanne d'Arc. Amsterdam: Balans.

Hamburg, F. 1995.

"Positieve discriminatie leidt slechts tot nieuw onrecht", De Volkskrant, 12 May 1995.

Hamburg, F. 2012.

Waarom democratie. Almere: Parthenon.

Heering, J. 1948.

Johan Huizinga's religieuze gedachten. Lochem: De Tijdstroom.

Hobbins, D. 2012.

Jeanne d'Arc. Het proces. Amsterdam: Nieuw Amsterdam.

Holden, H.T. 1991.

The continuing Relevance of Clausewitz: Illustrated Yesterday and Today with Application to the 1991 Persian Gulf War.

http://www.globalsecurity.org/military/library/report/1991/HHT.htm. Accessed 28 February 2020.

Jansen, J.H. 1957.

"Von Clausewitz en onze tijd." In: Orgaan van de Vereniging ter beoefening van de Krijgswetenschap. 1956-1957. Number 3.

Jestice, P.G. 2008.

The Timeline of medieval Warfare. San Diego: Thunderbay Press.

Keeney, R.L. 1992.

Value-focused Thinking. Cambridge. Massachusetts: Harvard University Press.

Kotani, K. 2009.

Japanese Intelligence in World War II. Oxford: Osprey Publishing.

Liddell Hart, B.H. 1944.

Thoughts on War. London: Faber and Faber.

Lucas, J. (ed.). 1988. Command. From Alexander the Great to Zhukov and the greatest Commanders of World History. London: Bloomsbury Publishing.

MacDonald, A.J.

"Courage, Fear and the Experience of the later medieval Scottisch Soldier." In: The Scottish historical Review 1992 (2), p.179/206. http://www.euppublishing.com/toc/shr/92/2. Accessed 28 February 2020.

Manning, S. 2010.

Joan of Arc's military Successes and Failures. http://www.scottmanning.com/content/joan-of-arc-military-successes-and-failures/. Accessed 28 February 2020.

Mantel, P.G. 1931.

Inleiding tot de leer der oorlogsvoering. Breda: De Koninklijke Militaire Academie.

Martin, M.M. 1989.

Présence de Jeanne d'Arc. Paris: O.E.I.L.

Montgomery, B.L. 1961.

The Path to Leadership. London: Collins.

Nester, W.R. 2012.

Napoleon and the Art of Diplomacy. New York: Savas Beatie.

Newman, J.R. 1942.

The Tools of War. New York: Doubleday.

Péguy, C. 1951.

Le Mystère de la Charité de Jeanne d'Arc. NRF, Le Rayon d'Or.

Pernoud, R. 1962.

Jeanne d'Arc par elle-même et par ses témoins. Paris: Éditions du Seuil.

Pernoud, R. & M.V. Clin. 2011.

Jeanne d'Arc. Paris : Pluriel.

Poortenaar, J. 1949 (?).

Jeanne d'Arc. Naarden: In den Toren.

Rees, L. 2013.

Het charisma van Adolf Hitler. Amsterdam: Ambo.

Rehabilitation. Procès de condamnation et de réhabilitation de Jeanne d'Arc, dite La Pucelle. Also known as Nullification or Rehabilitation. https://www.jeanne-darc.info/trial-of-nullification/ 01-13. Accessed 30 July 2020.

Richey, S.W. 2000.

Joan of Arc. A military appreciation. http://www.stjoan-center.com/military/stephenr.html. Accessed 28 February 2020.

Roberts, E. 2011.

Jeanne d'Arc: Morale, Spiritual Authority, and Gunpowder. https://www.medievalists.net/2011/05/jeanne-darc-morale-spiritual-authority-and-gunpowder/. Accessed 28 February 2020.

Rooyen, Van J.J. 2013.

Les traverses du pouvoir. Cadillac: ESR.

Seward, D. 2003.

The Hundred Years War. London: Robinson.

Shaw, B. 1934.

Saint Joan. Leipzig: Bernhard Taugnitz.

Sibley R. & M.Fry. 2008.

Erwin Rommel. Woestijnvos van het Afrika Korps. Hilversum: Just Publishers.

Slim, W. 1958.

Defeat into Victory. London: Landsborough publications.

Spoto, D. 2007.

Joan. The mysterious Life of the Heretic who became a Saint. New York: HarperCollins.

Stolpe, S. 1949.

Jeanne d'Arc. Utrecht, Antwerp: Het Spectrum.

Taylor, L.J. 2010.

The Virgin Warrior. The Life and Death of Joan of Arc. New Haven: Yale University Press.

Thomas, H. 2000.

Jungfrau und Tochter Gottes. Berlin: Alexander Fest Verlag.

Tuchman, B. 1982.

De waanzinnige 14e eeuw. Amsterdam/Brussels: Elsevier.

Virion, P. 1972.

Le Mystère de Jeanne d'Arc et la politique des nations. Téqui. Second edition.

Vlasboom, D.

"De mythische gedaanten van de Middeleeuwen." In: NRC Weekend, 24 September & 25 September, 2011. [Interview with Peter Raeds, author of 'De ontdekking van de Middeleeuwen – Geschiedenis van een illusie'.]

Vrijsen, E. 2014.

West-Europa leeft in fantasie.

https://www.elsevierweekblad.nl/buitenland/news/2014/08/veiligheidsexpert-west-europa-leeft-in-fantasie-1579185W/. Accessed 28 February 2020.

Warner, M. 2000.

Joan of Arc. The Image of female Heroism. Berkeley: University of California Press.

Wheeler-Bennett, J.W. 1954.

The Nemesis of Power. London: MacMillan.

Williams, C. 2005.

Pétain. New York: Palgrave MacMillan.

Wing, R.L (transl.). 1988. Sun Tzu.

The Art of Strategy. New York: Doubleday.

Winwar, F. 1948.

Jeanne d'Arc. Antwerp: De Nederlandse Boekhandel.

Yukl, G. 1998.

Leadership in Organisations. New Jersey: Prentice Hall.

Additional consulted websites:

http://www.jeanne-darc.info

http://www.maidofheaven.com/joanofarc_guy_de_laval.asp

www.ingramcontent.com/pod-product-compliance
Lightning Source LLC
LaVergne TN
LVHW041711070526
838199LV00045B/1294